Get Thee to a Bakery

Get Thee to a Bakery

Essays / Rick Bailey

University of Nebraska Press / *Lincoln*

For Kristin, with appreciation—

Rick Bailey

Library of Congress Cataloging-in-Publication Data
Names: Bailey, Richard, 1952– author.
Title: Get thee to a bakery: essays / Rick Bailey.
Description: Lincoln: University of Nebraska
Press, [2021]
Identifiers: LCCN 2020025984
ISBN 9781496225511 (paperback)
ISBN 9781496225610 (epub)
ISBN 9781496225627 (mobi)
ISBN 9781496225634 (pdf)
Subjects: LCSH: Bailey, Richard, 1952– | Bailey,
Richard, 1952—Travel. | Older men—United
States—Biography. | Authors, American—21st
century—Biography. | College teachers—United
States—Biography. | Food habits. | Global envi-
ronmental change.
Classification: LCC CT275.B225 A3 2021 |
DDC 920—dc23
LC record available at
https://lccn.loc.gov/2020025984

Set in Questa by Mikala R. Kolander.

For Gabriel and Silas

Contents

Get Thee to a Bakery

1 / Get Thee to a Bakery

"I wish you wouldn't do that," my wife says.

It's a sunny Saturday morning, early September. I'm climbing a ladder leaned up against the house. It's that time of year. The air has begun to change; it's both crisp and faintly rotten smelling. Where we live, we are rich in cottonwoods, proving that riches can also be a curse. Trees with big leaves, cottonwoods start unleaving early in the fall. Our cottonwoods are mature, tall beasts. The gutters on the house are already full. Up on the ladder, I'm on clog patrol.

"Really," she says.

I tell her I'm being careful.

Some years ago, Lowell, one of her pals from work, fell off a ladder and broke his back. Then Bill, the neighbor down the street, fell off a ladder and hurt his shoulder. My brother once said, right in front of my wife, that he thought a person ought to be required to have a license to climb a ladder, much like they need a license to drive a car or carry a gun. Ladders, he said, are that dangerous. He was kidding, but only just a little. Around that time our father, standing a rung higher than he thought he was, stepped prematurely off a ladder into low midair and collided with the cement floor of the garage. For weeks he was black and blue and walked with a limp.

My wife points at my feet. "In flip-flops, no less." She shakes her head and stalks back into the house.

"When I'm done here," I call after her, "I'm going to reward myself with a piece of pumpkin pie."

One of America's greatest gifts to itself, pumpkin pie can be traced to the Plymouth Plantation, where the original locals turned the Pilgrims on to pumpkins. Linda Stradley's *What's Cooking America* illustrates this lineage, describing a primitive confection of stewed pumpkin and a hollowed-out pumpkin shell filled with honey, milk, and spices, cooked in ashes.

Food historians point to how quickly pumpkins and pumpkin cooking proliferated back in Europe. As early as 1651, recipes for pumpkin pie were already being published. I give you François-Pierre de La Varenne, for example, and his *Le cuisinier françois*, with a recipe for tourte of pumpkin. "Boile it with good milk, pass it through a straining pan very thick, and mix it with sugar, butter, a little salt and if you will, a few stamped almonds; let all be very thin. Put it in your sheet of paste; bake it. After it is baked, besprinkle it with sugar and serve." I would eat that.

The Colonial Williamsburg Foundation's podcast, *Past & Present*, reports that the first American cookbook was published in 1796 and includes two recipes for a pumpkin pudding, one remarkably similar to the pie recipe used today: the pumpkin was "cooked with cream, eggs, sugar, mace, nutmeg, and ginger, and baked . . . three quarters of an hour in a crust." This recipe, the podcast notes, anticipates the one on the label of the Libby pumpkin can.

Early in our marriage, my wife the purist stated her intentions: she would make pumpkin pie from an actual pumpkin. While I know I should have been seduced by her desire to do so, I was not. I am a can man. My mother got her pumpkin from a can. For me, until recently, her pie was the gold standard.

"I know about pumpkin," my wife said. "In Italy we have pumpkin ravioli. Pumpkin is not just an American thing."

What can I say? I stand by the can.

This time of year, if you know the poem, you want to quote it. "Margaret, are you grieving / Over Goldengrove unleaving?" I would say this line to my wife today—she knows and loves the poem—if it weren't for the ladder and the part about grieving.

Of course she's right about one thing. (Correction: she's right about many things.) Climbing a ladder in flip-flops adds idiotic to reckless. I tell myself I'm careful. When I climb down from a ladder, I try to clear my mind of everything but this: Step. Step. Step. A slow, deliberate descent. This morning, half respecting her wishes, I climb down and walk around the house to the garage, thinking about autumn and wanwood leaf meal and pumpkin pie. I take a seat by the back door and tie on a pair of running shoes I've disgraced by wearing when I mow the lawn.

When she comes out to check on me later, I'm up on the ladder by the front door, dragging damp leaves into a pile along a length of gutter, leaning as far as I can safely lean to reach a clot of leaves. I straighten up, hold out a foot. "See?"

"Better."

I ask her what the word for *nutmeg* is in Italian.

"Don't lean so far," she says. "That's how you fall."

One of the ways, I think.

"It's like you have a fall wish," she says.

A fall wish. Maybe so. Whenever I'm up there, I think about stretching out the lean a little too far, the ladder sliding away and out from under me, leaving me dangling by one arm from the gutters or, worse, falling to the ground like an overripe fruit. In the plunge, would the ferns and hostas break my fall? I imagine myself landing safely, a soft bounce on a cushion of green leaves and fragrant mulch and dry cottonwood leaves.

"*Nutmeg* in Italian," she says over her shoulder, "is *noce moscata.*"

This time of year, Costco cranks up the pumpkin pie assembly line. From September to Thanksgiving, you can get an ample pie, a full twelve inches in diameter, with a deep rich filling and an adequate crust. It's the only time of year we buy a pie.

In bouts of parsimonious trimming every other day or so, often at night an hour or so before bed, we shamelessly indulge in narrow slivers and slices. She leaves the crust; I eat everything. A pie lasts ten days to two weeks. Then we go back for another. It's seasonal. We tell ourselves we would be crazy not to enjoy one, or many, much like when we are in San Marino in November, the month of the dead, we eat *piada dei morti*, a round honey-glazed "bread of the dead" made with flour, grape must, walnuts, almonds, and dried fruits. A *piada dei morti* lasts about as long as a pumpkin pie. We can't eat just one.

For me, after pumpkin, what makes a pumpkin pie a pumpkin pie is nutmeg. *Noce moscata*. *Noce*, nut. Got that. What's *moscata*?

Nutmeg is a spice with a long history, whose place of origin is the Banda Islands (a.k.a. Spice Islands) in Indonesia. There are early references to the Romans using nutmeg as incense; to the Byzantine monk Saint Theodore Studites encouraging monks to sprinkle it on pease pudding (think bean soup); to the Elizabethans using it as a defense against the plague. In the nineteenth century, nutmeg was believed to induce abortion and psychosis. Something as powerful as nutmeg also acquires minor curative capabilities: relief from pain, help for insomnia, a digestive aid. It's good for brain health, good for skin and for circulation, a remedy for bad breath. And, briefly noted: From earliest recorded history to the present, nutmeg has been valued as an aphrodisiac. The Louise M. Darling Biomedical Library at UCLA notes references to nutmeg in the *Kama Sutra*. In a 2009 Urban Dictionary entry, we learn, thanks to nutmeg, no doubt, that "pumpkin pie is the best aphrodisiac" (this according to a field scientist whose screen name is MyDickCostTheLateNightFee).

Nutmeg, I learn, came to Italy through Venice, from the trade routes into the Oman city of Muscat. Hence, *moscata*.

The Italians put nutmeg in ravioli, in tortellini; in my wife's region it's in *passatelli*, which is a bread crumb, egg, and parmigiano mix extruded into delicate fragrant worms you eat in broth or lightly sauced. I recently scanned recipes for ragù Bolognese in *La cucina italiana*. In almost all entries, nutmeg is an ingredient. In Italian cuisine, writes Cristina Gambarini, and most especially throughout Emilia-Romagna, "la noce moscata trovò la sua terra d'elezione." Roughly translated: Nutmeg found its home.

I might fall. I won't fall.

I just might fall.

"We are all one little slip," our neighbor says one day, "a thoughtless moment, a stupid move, a lapse in attention, from real trouble." It's not Bill, the neighbor who fell off the ladder. This is another neighbor, whose husband has reached falling age. His falls are of the perfunctory variety, ordinary moments of imbalance and crash in the kitchen or bathroom. Then again, no fall is ordinary. A fall fractures our illusion of continuation. It is also an ordinary thing. I can still do this. I still can climb the ladder. But maybe I shouldn't.

The cottonwoods, then the maples, then the apple trees will fill the gutters with leaves through December.

I probably shouldn't.

Today, putting away the ladder and thinking about pie, when I consider falling, I picture the pre-Raphaelite Ophelia. It's sort of how I would like to go: down into a bed of ferns and hostas, into wanwood leaf meal, or better, down into a large pumpkin pie, with the fragrance of nutmeg rising around me, lifting me toward heaven.

2 / This Body Offers to Carry Us

"It smells like worms out here," my wife says.

It's the beginning of October. We're coming out of a small grocery store in a light rain one morning. We are not loaded with bags. We've bought just one item. Reaching the car, we pull open the doors. She's on her side, I'm on mine. The doors swing open and we turn, balancing ourselves on one leg, then bend, lean, fold, and carefully lower our bodies onto our respective seats. As we do this, both of us emit very audible, slightly embarrassing, simultaneous groans.

What was that? I think.

"What was that?" she says to herself.

Is there such a thing as groan harmony?

Later that day, because I'm listening for it now, I hear both of us heave luxurious solo groans. When I bend to tie a pair of shoes by the back door. When she lifts herself out of a chair in the living room. When I take a pan out a cupboard in the kitchen. When she reaches into the back of a closet for an orphan shoe.

That night I steady myself against the bed and start pulling off a pair of jeans that are just tight enough to require some effort. It's not a difficult job. I'm not exactly shuffling off this mortal coil of mine. But again comes the groan.

When did this start? I wonder. And why? We exercise, we are not overweight, we are not old exactly. Just beginning to incline . . . old-ward. But there it is, the age-related groan.

No, the wheels aren't falling off, but they have begun to wobble. Standing at the bathroom sink one night, brushing my teeth, I hear my wife say, "I thought it was spine. But I guess it's just muffins."

"What?" I say around my toothbrush. Over the hum of the device and the splash of water running in the sink, I can't hear her. Increasingly, I admit, I can't hear her, even when there's less circumambient noise. Like the groan, not hearing well is also now a thing.

"Yoga," I hear her say.

I'm rinsing carefully, trying to keep cold water away from a molar. Yoga. And muffins? I spit, turn to her, and say, "Muffins?"

"Muscles," she says, with just a touch of pique. "I said *muscles*. The source of my back pain. It's not spine. It's muscles. Why are you making that face?"

"This tooth," I tell her. "I have to go back to your dentist."

She rolls her eyes.

I shut off the bathroom light, pull back the covers, and climb into bed, doing my best to enter and achieve a comfortable prone position without a decibel of age-related groan.

I search around the molar with my tongue. "So much for your dentist," I say.

We both know we are on the edge of a precipice. We take up our books and read, studiously ignoring each other.

For years now my wife and I have engaged in what might be called the dentist wars. I had my dentist; she had hers. Mine charged a little more than hers did. My wife would say a lot more. Her dentist was holistic. I would say kind of nutty. I asked one day, Does he fill your cavities with vitamins?

Every six months or so, around appointment time, we talked smack about the other's practitioner, lobbing fusillades of derision and contempt at each other. Dentists were good for our teeth; they were not good for our marriage. Our children worried about us. If we didn't watch ourselves, we could bicker at any time, in public, among friends, a loss of self-control as embarrassing as an age-related groan.

Eventually I did the math. My dentist did charge more, to the point of too much more. So, with some difficulty, I declared peace and went, finally, to her guy.

We started with a routine cleaning that day, me and the hygienist. It was fine. She used a power scaler, sonic blasting away at the plaque. Squirting around my mouth for detritus, she said something about biofilm and bacteria, assuring me that I was rinsing with ozone water, a good disinfectant and good for oxidation.

Then the dentist looked at my teeth.

My dentist always used to compliment my mouth. Poking around in there, she would say that things looked good, that I had a beautiful mouth. She made both of us feel good. This guy just nodded and said, at the end of his exam, that maybe I would want to redo some fillings, and there was a crown that ought to be replaced. My gums had pockets back there.

I thought I had a perfectly good crown, but pockets are pockets. That way lies bone decay. I also thought, Okay, give the guy a chance. At my next appointment, six months later, I consented to the crown job.

Tonight, as always, my wife is reading a book in bed, this one about Leonardo da Vinci and his saucy little friend Salaì. She gives me frequent reports, reading aloud in Italian and chuckling.

Tonight, as she often does, she tells me I really should read it. Whatever she's reading, I should read it too. *I dubbi di Salaì.* She says it's "kind of a historical, epistolary, satirical whodunit, set in Rome in 1501."

I hold up my Kindle. "Lots of one-syllable words in the book I'm reading, words I've never seen before. *Bleb*, for example."

"Right now," she says, "Salaì is making fun of one of Leonardo's flying machines. It's hilarious."

"Do you know what a bleb is?"

"English," she says, "has a lot more one-syllable words than Italian."

"How about a tot?"

"A small child."

"'A tot of booze' is how it's used," I say. "Maybe it's Irish English."

She says she heard somewhere that dyslexia is more common to speakers and readers of English than Italian because there are so many one-syllable words in English. She turns back to her book, an actual book, with a red hard cover and four-hundred-and-some actual pages you riffle. I tap my Kindle, returning to what I'm reading, Benjamin Black's *Even the Dead*. Also a whodunit, but without the Italian, historical, epistolary, satirical part.

It occurs to me, as we don't talk for a while, that lately I've been experiencing something like dyslexia. "I think I've got late-onset dyslexia," I say.

She gives her head a slight shake, which means "That's bull" or "Wait a sec" or both. She doesn't look up from her reading.

"The other day," I say, "I saw a sign on a store. I thought it said 'Enema.'"

With a slight groan, definitely not the age-related variety, she shuts her book and looks at me. "Really?"

"In giant letters, on the storefront, 'Enema.' It was actually 'Emma.' But I read 'Enema.'"

"That's just you."

"A few days ago, on a sign in that place we had breakfast, I read 'hurricane pies.'"

"Hurricane pies."

"Yes." I give her a minute. "Homemade," I say. "Homemade pies."

She nods a dismissive nod. A few minutes later, guarding against the groan, I reach for the lamp, switch off the light, and cast us into darkness.

"Bleb," I say.

"What is it?"

"It's like a blister."

To make and install a new crown is a routine procedure. First her dentist has to remove the old one, which involves numbing that area of my head and using a handheld motorized rotary saw to cut the thing into pieces. It takes a while, like ten or fifteen minutes. Time slows down during such procedures. Evidently my dentist spared no expense on material and adhesive. Hers was a crown for the ages.

Once that's done, we are both emotionally exhausted, and my brain is a little rattled. My wife's dentist quits the operating theatre, perhaps to go for an ozone water cocktail, while his assistant rolls a computer to the edge of my chair and fits a camera inside my mouth.

At this point in the original procedure, my dentist had shoved a huge wad of blue bubble gum back where my molar was and told me to bite down. Ten minutes later, the wad, beginning to harden, was extracted, enabling my dentist to make a temporary crown, which she referred to as a "tin can," which I found altogether charming. She then sent out the blue bubblegum form to a foundry somewhere, which built a crown for the ages. That took a week or so.

What's going on? I'd ask if I could. But I have a camera in my mouth.

I think the assistant says "cad-cam," but I could swear it's really "goddam." That's certainly my point of view. Cad-cam and on-site manufacturing. That's a lot of holistic dentistry from the standpoint of technology.

Half an hour later I have a brand-new polished porcelain crown. On the drive home I give it an inquisitive tonguing. It feels a little smaller than the other one. But a crown is a crown. Right?

I want to be right about this, I really do, but it would appear that a crown is not a crown. As feeling returns to that quadrant of my mouth I become aware of sensitivity to cold back there. When I take a drink of water, the only reasonable response is a wince and a groan.

I wait a week, protecting the crown, directing everything cold that I eat or drink to the opposite quadrant. Which is kind of ridiculous. In the modern mouth, all lanes should be open to traffic.

A week passes.

"Amish children legs," I say to my wife.

We're lying in bed reading. Every couple minutes or so, she laughs. Salaì is that funny. The guy in my book, an aging pathologist named Quirke, who works in the Dublin morgue, is trying to control his drinking and solve a crime. He's not funny.

"What?" she says.

"It's what I read the other day, on a sign. 'Amish children legs.'"

She's having a hard time pulling herself back from Rome in 1501, back to the present, back to my nonsense. "What?" she says. "What are you talking about?"

"My dyslexia? It's what I read today. 'Amish children legs.' Instead of 'Amish chicken legs.'"

She's exasperated, and I kind of love that.

"I also read something funny online this morning," I tell her. "I thought it said 'You can get drunk for free this Friday at Starbucks.' How about that?"

"What did it really say?"

"I don't know. Maybe 'free donuts'? Personally, I would rather get drunk at Starbucks. And this afternoon I thought you said you wanted to buy some more handles."

"When was that?"

"HomeGoods. Candles. You said 'candles.' But I heard 'handles.' That's like auditory dyslexia."

"No," she says, "you just need to get a hearing aid." She gives me a ponderous look that says: Do something about your hearing loss. Be proactive. The look also says: Make my life a little easier. In truth, I sometimes like hearing things wrong.

I tell her I have to go back to her dentist. I've waited a week. I've tried not to complain. Our truce in the dentist wars holds, but barely.

"Sometimes I can't use one side of my mouth."

She says he'll fix me up.

Right. It's nothing a little holistic high tech can't fix.

I go. He doesn't fix me up. Back in the chair, I explain—I try not to sound like I'm complaining, but isn't this situation complain-worthy?—I report that I can't let anything cold near the crown. I open, he looks, I close. He says it's inflammation. He says I'll need the low-level laser treatment.

His assistant gives me the LLLT. In a few minutes I'm out of there. Days, weeks, months pass. No change. I weigh my options: go back for the handheld motorized rotary saw or wait patiently. I decide to wait.

The big red book lies slightly askew in her hands that night in bed. She might be sleeping.

"Singles vaccination," I say. "How about that?"

"What?"

"A sign I saw. It said 'shingles'; I saw 'singles.' And here's another one: 'Cuvee Turd.'" She doesn't engage on this one. I don't know what word *turd* was supposed to be. Nor do I care. I just want to savor the absurdity.

"Can you reach my bookmark?" she says. "I think it slipped under the bed."

I get out of bed, walk around to her side, get down on my hands and knees, and look. Yep, there it is. As I get back to my feet, I let go a long, satisfying age-related groan. Those groaning tennis players come to mind; weight lifters and prizefighters, they groan. I hand her the bookmark, get back in bed, shut off the light. In a few minutes her breathing slows. If she were awake, and if I were good at memorizing poetry, I would recite these lines for her, from a Robert Bly poem: "My friend, this body offers to carry us for nothing—as the ocean carries logs. So on some days the body wails with its great energy; it smashes up the boulders, lifting small crabs, that flow around the sides."

Maybe once my body wailed with great energy, possibly it still does on rare occasions. Increasingly I think of my body as a vintage car carrying me through life, rust spots, soft tires, cracked windshield, indicator lights on the dash that flash on and off, indicating nothing.

The Bly reference to the ocean reminds me of a sign I misread. Public snore. I'll have to share that one with my wife tomorrow night. Give her a minute to guess before I tell.

3 / A Minor Memory

I've been using *Shazam* as a verb for a while now.

Not to be confused with the interjection that expresses amazement Gomer Pyle–style. It's when I use the Shazam app on my phone. It'll name that tune.

Open the app and touch its signature icon to begin Shazaming. The app "listens." You see concentric circles radiating outward the way submarine sonar looked in old TV programs and black-and-white movies. Shazam decodes the music's digital signal, searches databases, and, shazam! You're listening to Vashti Bunyan's "Train Song" or Bach's Prelude and Fugue in C Minor.

Since I've begun Shazaming, I've stood in noisy bars and restaurants with my hand raised, my phone pointed in the direction of the music coming from speakers in the ceiling, waiting for the app to Shazam what I'm listening to. In the old days, you might ask a server or proprietor, "What song is this?" In the old days, listening to the radio, you would wait for the song to end, wait for a DJ to say, "That was Stephen Martin's 'Three by Two' on his quartet's new LP entitled *Vision*." If she said it, that is. Big if. Sometimes you waited for the end of the song, waited through the next song, through a few commercials after that, coming up with nothing. Now, in the car, in a bar, almost anytime I hear music I don't recognize, I can thumb my device to life, touch the icon, and, well, shazam, it's "Are You That Somebody?" by Aaliyah.

"I'm going to ask Roxane if she Shazams," I say to my wife one day. She's reading the news on her device.

No response.

"What do you think?"

Her device is an iPad. She does not use a smartphone. She is not a good friend of computers. She has only basic operating knowledge of the TV remote and can't run the Roku. But her iPad, she depends on and loves. It is a faithful companion.

"Sure," she says without looking up. Then, "Wait, what?" Now she lifts her gaze, but just barely. "I don't know. What are you talking about?"

"Are you reading the news?"

"Yes. What is it? What did you ask me just now?"

"You were phnubbing me," I say.

"What?"

"You're phnubbing me. It's a new word. You put *phone* and *snubbing* together, you get phnubbing."

"Stop saying these things to me when I'm trying to read."

"I'm going to ask Roxane if she Shazams."

She shakes her head, goes back to her reading.

The portmanteau is actually *phubbing*. Kevin Roose, writing for the *New York Times*, recently described his new tech regimen, which involves devoting significantly less time to tech. He says he spends more time reading, more time pondering, more time listening to his wife, "less time distractedly nodding and mumbling while checking my inbox or tapping out tweets."

Less time phubbing the people he cares about.

Phubbing is the real word—a neologism that will probably die young. I prefer *phnubbing*.

"Well, I'm going now," I say to my wife.

She's tapping her device when I leave. So many taps. Solitaire, I would guess by the sound of her taps. When I get to the back door, from deep in the house I hear, "Bye."

Roxane lives down the street. She's given piano lessons to every kid in the neighborhood, our kids included. And me included. She's an eightysomething who recently lost her husband. These days, on occasional visits, I take her my musical questions. I thought of her a few days ago when I heard a piece of music. I was in the car on a Sunday morning, making a run to the store for milk. Local FM was playing Beethoven's Seventh Symphony. I didn't need to Shazam it.

I called Roxane when I got home.

"I know that music," I said to her. "They did something funny in the second movement." I hummed the phrasing.

She said, "Yes?"

"Do you know it?"

She made a choking sound. Her way of saying "Duh."

I said I'd never heard it like that before. The phrasing seemed rushed, compared to the recording I've listened to on and off since 1971, when I took music appreciation in college. I hummed the phrase twice, the 1971, then the 2019 version. Would a conductor, I asked, make an interpretive decision about that phrasing?

"It's certainly possible," she said. "There's so much variety in the scores, as they are written and printed over time. Mozart might leave a few notes off here and there. Ravel is notorious. Then, over decades and centuries, printing, you know, the blanks are filled in. And there's human error."

I hummed the melody one more time. "I bet it's in A minor," I said.

"Listen," she said, "why don't you come down next week and we'll look at some music together."

So this afternoon I walk down the street to her house—the way I did years ago, once a week, for a year of lessons, remembering the nerves, my performance anxiety. I didn't practice enough. I didn't read well. I couldn't open my hands. I sat next to her and played, feeling like Gomer Pyle.

She's waiting. Once I get seated in the kitchen, she makes us instant coffee in the microwave, cuts slices of yellow cake. She's still getting used to being alone. She worries about falling. The stairs terrify her. We move down the agenda of neighborly topics: squirrels, snow removal, her kids, mine. The change in the neighborhood. People aren't as friendly. She says she has only six students now. The serious ones. It's enough.

Her grand piano is in the next room. She's made a pile of music on the dining room table for us to look at. A Brahms sonata, two charts, one of which she says she played when she was a girl. She opens both on the piano.

"See," she says, pointing to one chart, then the other. "*Piano* here; *forte* there. Same measure." She opens up a couple Mozarts. "*Diminuendo* here; on this piece, same place, nothing." We go through a few more examples. I'd like her to play the Brahms; I ask if she still plays it. She says yes but does not volunteer. Back at the dining room table, she shows me a beautifully ornate book, a collection of the Mozart concertos. She pushes a box of CDs toward me, all the Beethoven symphonies. "Take these," she says. "I don't need them back."

She also hands me sheet music for Beethoven's Fifth, written for piano. It actually says "made easy for piano." Kids' stuff. It's the thought that counts.

"You can play this," she says. "You know Beethoven's Fifth?"

I make a choking sound. Her way of saying "Duh!"

"Take this too." She hands me an old hardcover book, *Beethoven the Creator* by Romain Rolland. She opens it and turns to the page where there is a small flowing handwritten inscription in black ink. "To my dear friend and pupil. December 25, 1929." "My mother's piano teacher gave her this book," she says. "My mother gave it to me. It's precious. I'll want it back."

As I'm leaving we talk for a minute more at the front door, a little sostenuto. "You know it is A minor, that second movement," she says, meaning that second movement of Beethoven's Seventh. "How did you know? Pitch memory?"

I have to thank Top Ten radio. When I was in seventh grade and learning to play the guitar, like every beginner, I played "House of the Rising Sun," made famous by Eric Burdon and the Animals. The song began with an A minor arpeggio on the electric guitar.

That sighing, mournful opening chord of the second movement of Beethoven's Seventh, I knew, was in the same key.

That night I'm washing a couple dishes, and I ding a bowl with a wooden spoon. It rings a distinctive, unmistakable note. My gosh, I think, it's gotta be E.

To check this, I try to recall a song in the key of E major: the opening chords to "Gloria" by Them (the Them, I like to say now), in the summer of 1964. "Let me tell you about my baby . . ."

I'm singing it now, finishing the dishes. "She comes around . . ."

There must be an app that can listen and report out. You hum a note, whack a cereal bowl, the app listens and says "That's B flat." Later I'm googling around on my iPhone looking for such an app when I see my wife, curled up on the end of the sofa, reading her *Salaì*. A real book. She's reading a book.

She looks up and smiles. Her look says, Who's phnubbing whom? Her look says it, but I know she would never use that word.

"So how was your visit with Roxane?" she says.

"It was really good," I say. "She's chatty. I came away with gifts."

"She must be lonely."

"She has her students," I say. "But yes, I think she is."

I show her the Beethoven symphonies, Roxane's mother's book. I tell her how good it felt visiting this older person, with her deep knowledge of music, her curiosity and wit, her perfect pitch.

"Does she?" my wife asks.

"What?"

"Does Roxane say Shazam?"

I smile and tell her I forgot to even mention it. Next time I have an urgent musical question, next visit, I will. And soon.

4 / *Con te partirò*

Plato, the evidence suggests, was nervous about music. He would have excluded the flute from the Republic. His vision of an ideal world was men (of course) standing around talking, engaged in dialectic, getting at the truth, making some wisdom. Music, and the flute in particular, would be distracting. He writes in the *Republic*: "When someone gives music an opportunity to charm his soul with the flute and pour those sweet, soft, and plaintive tunes we mentioned through his ear . . . after a time his spirit is melted and dissolved until it vanishes, and the very sinews of his soul are cut out."

That sounds bad. Sometime, somewhere, you're going to need those soul sinews.

The term probably didn't exist in Greek, but I think what Plato had in mind was *earworm*. Music, he knew, gets inside your head.

I've had a bad case of earworm for about a week. Without meaning to, totally against my will, I find myself humming Andrea Bocelli's "Con te partirò." Not humming it. What's going on is more like think-hum. Earworm. It's vivid and involuntary, silent and persistent.

I've got nothing against Andrea Bocelli. I'm sure he's a very nice guy. But I've heard this song far too many times, in all kinds of circumstances, mostly weddings but also in a lot of restaurants. If there's a place where love is in the air or that makes use of or projects Italian culture, "Con te partirò'" will be there.

I mentioned it to my wife a couple days ago, humming that distinctive line in the song, *na-na-na na-na-na na-na-na-na nahhhhhh.*

"Don't do that," she says.

"He only has that one song."

She says there are lots of songs.

"Name one."

"Whole albums full of songs."

"Yes, but that's the one that gets you," I say. "It's like Elvis Presley. 'You ain't nothin' but a hound dog.'"

"Just don't hum it."

"Or Tiny Tim, 'Tiptoe through the Tulips.'"

She shakes her head.

"'Con te partirò,'" I say, "is Andrea Bocelli's 'Tiptoe through the Tulips.'"

The other senses aren't wormy the way hearing is. Take smell, for instance. There's baked bread and lilac and gasoline, powerful smells that set your olfactory receptors atingle, but those scents and fragrances and stinks don't visit you, unbidden, when you're taking a shower or walking down the street. Or consider the tactile sense. The last couple mornings, to keep from waking my wife, I've gone for coffee at a place called Happy Donuts in San Francisco, just down the street from our hotel, earworming Bocelli as I go. At 5:00 a.m. in Happy Donuts it's just me and a couple homeless people and a thin, stoic Chinese guy. Everyone asleep sitting up. I lean against a table the first morning, with bare arms, and feel the unmistakable cling of a sticky surface: spilled soft drink, a smear of icing, maybe something worse. That surface delivers a sensory impression that makes an impression. But unlike earworm, it has the decency not to come back and stay awhile, revisiting you when you least want it or expect it.

We're finishing a long stint of sightseeing. These weeks I've seen buttes and mesas, cliff faces and canyons, rushing streams and waterfalls. Yesterday we stood in front of the amazing murals in Coit Tower. Today I can conjure faces of cliffs or the faces we saw at Coit Tower if I want to. I can pick up a piece of pizza, fold it in half, raise it to my mouth—and sort of see images, while in the background of my mind I hear Bocelli singing *na-na-na na-na-na na-na-na-na nahhhhhh.* Unlike earworm, images don't come at me out of nowhere and hang around. There's no such thing as eye worm.

According to *Psychology Today*: "Well over 90% of people report having an earworm at least once a week." In psychological literature there is reference to involuntary musical imagery.

Help, if you want to call it that, exists. There's an app for that, of course. Unhearit. It's a new website that uses "the latest in reverse-auditory-melodic-unstickification technology." Upon further investigation, however, it sounds like you just swap a new earworm for an old one. Out goes "Con te partirò." In comes "The Chicken Dance."

It occurs to me that I have no idea what exactly Bocelli is singing about. If it's going to be lodged in my head, I think I ought to find out. One of my first hits on a "Con te partirò" Google search takes me to Tranquility Burial and Cremation Services. Okay, now I'm plundering my memory. Have I heard that song at a funeral? Ever?

Never.

Partirò. It's a song about leave-taking. The lyrics seem to swing both ways, end of life, beginning of life. You're giving away your daughter at her wedding. It's the end of her life with you, the beginning of her life with him (or her). Or, hey, we may be breaking up, but we'll always have that great time together in Cleveland. Or, one of us really is, like, dead.

I just might pay Unhearit a visit. I've spent way too much time with "Con te partirò." My soul sinews are stretched to the breaking point.

5 / On Wine Tasting and the
Limits of Winespeak

"You taste wine the same way I do," the guy pouring says. "We all have the same equipment: nose, mouth, tongue, palate."

Technically, yes. And it's nice of him to say that.

It's my last day in Sonoma. I've had a head cold all week, so none of my "equipment" has been working very well. Thus far I've had only a few sips of wine with lunches and dinners. This afternoon I've decided to visit some tasting rooms, to open my mouth and let the wine in. There are over 425 wineries in Sonoma County, fifteen or so within a few miles of where I'm staying. This one is known for its chardonnays and pinots.

I've just tasted the third of three pinot noirs the winery is pouring today, and listened, amazed, to the wine guy's description of the wine, a brief disquisition on its body (medium), its structure (supple), acidity (tangy), fruit (cherry pie), spice (an allspice matrix!), barrel time (old French oak), tannins (pliable), and finish (persistent).

"I don't taste cherry," I say.

Nor do I detect structure. I understand *tannin* but I don't get *pliable*. I tell him my mouth is dumb. I'm just not a very good taster.

He asks, "Did you like it?"

"Yes, I did," I say, and empty my glass into the spittoon.

On a scale of 0–3, 0 being never again, 3 being bring it on, I'd give this wine a 2.

These wines probably have Parker Points and *Wine Spectator* ratings, both of which use a 100-point scale. Suppose the wine you're tasting is a 92. I wonder: What would make it a 91? A little less pliability? What would make it a 93? A slightly larger slice of cherry pie? This may be an example of effing in ineffable. How do you quantify a qualitative judgment?

Eons ago, as an undergraduate in a survey of twentieth-century British literature, I wrote a midterm essay in response to this assignment: "Referring to at least two of the authors we've read in the course thus far, analyze the nature of metaphor in modern literature. What, specifically, are the metaphors in, say, Conrad and Yeats? If the metaphors are vehicles for their ideas, what are the limits of metaphoric expression?"

Fortunately, or maybe unfortunately, it was a take-home test. Over the weekend I thought hard about "the nature of metaphor in modern literature," thought about it until my head hurt. I pored over a handful of Yeats poems, with helpful annotations I had made, like these: "Cycle of time. A vision of hope. Mutability of experience. The body." I reread my marginal notes on *Heart of Darkness*—"Knitters of fate. Categories of defense. The failure of language. Existential challenge"—all the while trying to figure out exactly what "the limits of metaphoric expression" might mean. I wrote, I returned to my notes and annotations, I revised and gradually stopped writing. My essay had a long finish.

Next class I handed in three closely written pages and waited a week for the professor to return my work. When I got it back, I found a few phrases of my essay underlined, a few phrases double underlined, along with an occasional question mark and a few trenchant exclamation marks in the margin. Flipping to the last page, as we all do, I looked for the grade. It was an 87. I knew what that meant, a B. Okay, but 87? How had he arrived at that specific number, and not, let's say, 86 or 88? Those underlines and double underlines, did they add to or subtract from 100? What could I have done, what exactly was he looking for that would have made my essay an 89 or 90? I suspect he might not have been able to explain how he arrived at 87 or what I could do to raise that number to 88 or 90, beyond telling me something like "be smarter, make better connections."

A few years later, as a young teacher, I filled a grade book every semester with marks (I decided on A through E) for twenty-two students in each of the five classes I taught. Homework, quizzes, exercises, essays, midterms, finals. At semester's end, for each student, I would see something like this: C, A, B-, B+, B-, D, E, A-, A-, C+, C+, C, B+, A-, E, E, B, B, B. To arrive at a final grade, I laid a ruler across each row of marks, tracking student performance left to right, across fifteen weeks, and on the far right rendered my final judgment: B. Sometimes, upon further reflection, I affixed a minus or a plus to that letter. Never quite sure, except in my bones or in my heart or vaguely (very vaguely) in my head, if that grade with its plus or minus was a true value summarizing those letter grades.

This was long before the advent of spreadsheets and grading technologies, before primary trait analysis. And I'm pretty sure this grading practice was widespread: impressionistic, holistic, supported mainly by the authority of the individual who rendered the judgment. It was an 87 or a B+ because a full professor said it was. Enough said. Much like a pinot is a 92 because Robert Parker or *Wine Spectator* says it is.

Words help. They name qualities, characteristics. Words and categories enable dissection, which enables analysis and evaluation. The problem is, some things are easier to dissect than others.

I've been reading Walter Isaacson's biography of Leonardo da Vinci. Thanks to Isaacson's helpful descriptions of the great artist's paintings, I now look for Leonardo's use of shadow and *sfumatura*, for the characteristic depictions of water and hair and landscapes in his paintings. I imagine I see left-handed brush-strokes. Knowing something about Leonardo's work helps me see the paintings of other artists at the time differently. Huh, I might think, look at that pile of rocks. Did the artist even bother looking at nature the way Leonardo did? I get why his work breaks out of the 80s and rates in the high 90s.

As an undergraduate, even farther back than "the limits of metaphor," I took a music appreciation class. I must have listened to Mozart's Symphony no. 40 a hundred times. That symphony and that recording, by Sir Georg Solti conducting the Chicago Symphony Orchestra, established my frame of reference. I've been startled by other recordings of that symphony I've heard since, by how fast the first movement runs, by the chug and lurch of another conductor's minuet movement. I've listened to other symphonies with, well, enhanced appreciation, noticing how the second movement in no. 40 compares to the second movement in Mozart's no. 41 or, because of repeated, careful listening, how it compares to the amazing, mournful second movement in Beethoven's Seventh.

Seeing, listening, and tasting are not equal.

Seeing and listening lend themselves more readily to dissection and appreciation than tasting. A Leonardo just sits there, on the wall or on a page or a screen. Pull back from the artwork, or move in close, or alter the angle of your viewpoint. You can take a very long look. It's a freeze-frame experience. Likewise, in music: rewind, replay, revisit the same performance, the same shift to a major key, the swelling of sound, the crescendo. Listen, take it in. Looking carefully, listening intently, you can make the experience last as long as you like.

A taste, on the other hand, is brief, intense, and evanescent; a couple sips and it's finished. When you look and listen, you may get tired, but you don't get full. Or drunk. And what about memory? Are memories of what you see (a sunset, a face, a painting) and what you hear (a birdcall, a child's laugh, a piece of music) more retraceable and detailed and vivid than memories of a gustatory experience?

There are supertasters, I know, sipping savants in the wine world, people endowed with, if not supernatural equipment, then highly discriminating taste and deep stores of palate memory.

I bow to them. To communicate with us, they deploy a special language. They say things like this about wine: "Already revealing some pink and amber at the edge, the color is surprisingly evolved for a wine from this vintage. However, that's deceptive as the aromatics offer incredible aromas of dried flowers, beef blood, spice, figs, sweet black currants and kirsch, smoked game, lavender, and sweaty but attractive saddle leather-like notes. Full-bodied and massively endowed, with abundant silky tannins, it possesses the balance to age for 30+ years" (Robert Parker, on a 2001 Châteauneuf-du-Pape).

This is a pronouncement handed down from on high. It makes me want to taste the wine, but only after I've whiffed some beef blood and licked a sweaty saddle.

What sets the apprentice taster apart from the journeyman is years of experience and control of the language. Years ago a friend took me to his wine club dinner. A dozen men descended upon a restaurant (oh, yes, all men). Serious guys, they each brought their own box of Riedel glasses. It was an evening of blind tasting, eight wines chosen to accompany a nice dinner.

For two to three hours, we tasted wines in pairs and talked about them. Two amarones, for example, one a 2003, the other a 1999. I was given a notepad and pencil. After the pours we swirled and sniffed, sipped and deliberated. Then we went around the table and described the wines and our tasting experiences. Compared to these guys, I was still in short pants. "Full bodied," I could say. "Nice color." But they would have at it, making little speeches, practicing the lingo, somming it up. I went to three of these dinners. Every night I finished at the bottom of my class. And every night, the same two guys identified all the wines correctly. When they talked, I took notes. The older wines were tight. Some wines' tannins were grippy. They talked, but they didn't revel in winespeak.

Those nights I was reminded of graduate seminars I attended in which students, me included, practiced speaking lit crit, making statements like this: "Deconstructionists have to be aware of the text's shifts or breaks that may eventually create instabilities in attitude and meaning. At the verbal level, a close reading of the text will highlight its paradoxes and contradictions, a reading against the grain, in order to reveal how the 'signifiers' may clash with the 'signifieds.'"

Right.

Words help. They can explain the 87 and 92. They also can get in the way. Did you like it? Yes. Do you want to more? Yes.

Most of the time, that's enough.

6 / Learning to Like It

"Are you bringing the nuts?" my wife asks.

I hear the bowl ring as she pours out her granola. She's sitting at the kitchen table.

It's a mix we buy, part of our new health regimen, along with intermittent fasting. Our holistic doc has said, repeatedly, you can break the rules, you can abuse your body, until you're sixty. After that, to be in it for the long haul, you have to think about nutrition. So, some supplements. So, the nut mix that I'm sure we pay way too much for down at the farmers' market. "But they're fresh," my wife says. "But they're nuts," I say. We're on the eight plan. Loosely on it. "Eat eight vegetables a day," the doc says. "Eat within an eight-hour time period. Then fast."

I set the nut vat down in front of her, tell her no one has ever said that to me.

"You're having lunch with Jordan today?"

"Yes."

Jordan's a waiter friend of ours, a foodist, a winehead. Thirty years younger. "Don't drink too much," my wife says.

"I'll stop at just enough."

"You could stop before that." She tosses a handful of nuts on her granola. "No one's ever said what?"

"Are you bringing the nuts."

She looks at her bowl, stirring. I can tell she's waiting. I could make a joke. But I don't go there. I'm not totally predictable.

"We're going to Joe's," I say. "That bistro they have upstairs?"

"Was that Jordan's idea?"

"Mine. I don't know about the food, but we ought to find good parking."

"Get some crackers while you're there," she says. "Sweet potato and beet crackers."

"Both in the same bag?"

"No, two bags. Sweet potato crackers, orange; beet crackers, red."

Virtuous crackers, I think. How far we've traveled from saltines. I drop a handful of nuts on my Icelandic yogurt.

To get a head start on the eight plan, I drink a zucchini for breakfast.

Actually it's a vegetable cocktail. How do you ingest eight servings of vegetables a day? Here's how we do it. Our new gadget is the NutriBullet, a motorized mixer. Zucchini, broccoli florets, spinach, a celery stalk, a handful of fresh parsley. Whatever's green we have in the fridge, in it goes. And half a banana. Or a cup of blueberries. Add some organic water, and given a long spin and chop, you get a healthy greenish muck that goes down okay. Before 7:00 a.m. we're six vegetables to the good.

Pond scum, one of my friends calls it. "How's it taste?"

Not great. It can be bitter. But good bitter. I read somewhere that as you age, your taste buds begin to dull and die. Bitter becomes okay. Still, in the smoothie, fruit helps.

Easy on the fruit, health doc says. Lots of sugar.

"Enjoy your parking," my wife tells me later that morning.

I've called ahead to find out what time Upstairs Bistro opens.

Of all the Joes we have to choose from—Trader Joe's, Vince & Joe's, Joe's Produce, Joe's Gourmet, Joe's Liquor, Eat at Joe's—this Joe's is my least favorite. They've got the goods. But except for the vegetable man, there's a pervasive attitude problem. The guy who owns it, you can see him a hundred times, he walks by and looks right through you. The meat guys range from grouchy to misanthropic. How about an anger burger today? The cashiers,

I'm pretty sure they speak English, but beyond Paper or plastic?, they tend not to engage.

I get Laura on the phone. "We open at eleven," she says. "Shall I hold a table?"

These days I get my sugar from Beaujolais. It's not on the eight plan.

In the beginning, when I was learning to like wine, I couldn't like anything French. Probably because of price, probably because I couldn't make sense of the labels. When I decided to buy something French, I usually found myself standing at the checkout holding a bottle of bargain basement, under-ten-dollars Beaujolais. I paid no attention to dates. Later, when I tasted the wine at home, with the first sip I thought, Why don't I like this? What am I missing?

Then in the eighties, accompanied by an aggressive ad campaign, the Beaujolais nouveau became a much-ballyhooed thing. This was pre-internet. I read the Thursday *New York Times* wine column. One day, in an article that painted a colorful picture of wine harvest in France, of villages celebrating the new wine, I learned about nouveau. Now I too could celebrate the harvest with these young, vivacious wines.

Outside grocery stores you saw, on flowery, viney château-y signage, "Le nouveau est arrivé!" I was a D+ French student, but I could read that. So maybe I could also drink it. Maybe I could like it. But the below bargain-basement, under-nine-dollars nouveau tasted bad; not bad like other Beaujolais I had drunk. Those were just bad. This was young bad, a confusing sweetish fruit juice with an alcohol zing.

Was I also a D+ wine drinker?

At the top of the stairs at Bistro is a podium and a thin young woman with straight brown hair. She smiles and nods when she sees me. "Are you Laura?" I ask.

"Yes," she says brightly. "Are you Howard?"

How far I've traveled from Chris Cooper's house.

One summer day after sixth grade my friend Dan Leman and I rode our bikes out to Cooper's. In a cupboard above the kitchen sink, his father kept a fifth of vodka on the top shelf. I had never tasted anything alcoholic. My parents were teetotalers. Total. Chris poured a sip into the vodka bottle cap and handed it to Dan, who was very alcohol curious. He tasted it, winced, and held a pinched face. "It tastes like rotten toothpaste," he said.

I too was curious. But not quite ready.

On one hand, I have to think no one likes alcohol initially. You have to be motivated. My first taste of beer I was in ninth grade. My brother and two of his pals brought me along on a ski trip. They also brought along a case of Pabst Blue Ribbon. We spent the night at our family cottage. I had seen men with giant beer bellies lift longneck bottles to their mouths and upend them. I had heard my father talk warnfully about the dangers of drink. That night they handed me my own longneck. I couldn't finish even one bottle. It tasted terrible. Around two o'clock in the morning, the guy who had brought the beer threw up in my parents' bed.

Years later, newly married, I was out to dinner in Italy with my wife's friends. After the pasta and the grilled meats and the table wine, the gentleman said he would have grappa. A *digestivo*. Sure, I'd have one too, I said. I liked the word. What came to the table was clear, the color of lighter fluid. I had never tasted anything so foul. Eventually, after a decade of tasting and trying, I learned to like it, but not a lot. It took some work.

On the other hand, scientists think that humans must have a natural inclination, that they must be hard wired to drink alcohol. The desire to consume spirits is nearly universal across cultures. To explain that, there's a drunk-monkey hypothesis. Millions of years ago, when our ancestors climbed down from the trees, they prowled the jungles and savannahs where, attracted by the scent of fruit droppage fermenting on the ground, they gained both a blast of calories by way of sugars and a buzz from the ethanol content of what they ate. Robert Dudley, science writer for the *Atlantic*, refers to the "downwind vapor trail that reliably indicates the presence of fruits and sugars." We detect that.

I recall a scent like that, a moldy, yeasty vapor trail, wafting from the dark, and frightening, interior of the Log Cabin, one of our hometown bars. And then again later, there was the vapor trail in the Village Idiot, a bar that Dan and I, along with a few other drunk monkeys, made our home in Breckenridge, Colorado.

Now, when I've made sure no one is looking, I raise a glass of wine to my nose, swirl and sniff.

Laura hands me off to Michelle, who sets down two menus and wine list. There's no Beaujolais, which is okay with me. When Jordan sits down, he scans the list and suggests a Syrah or Rioja. Michelle brings a small glass of each for us to taste.

We go with the Rioja. Bottle.

Our Mediterranean grilled octopus comes with a generous sprinkling of arugula. The brussels sprout dish is served with white balsamic, red onion, truffle, and parmesan. When did I learn to like this stuff?

Two more vegetables.

I tell Jordan about the eight plan.

He asks: "Eight glasses of water too?"

No. I lift my glass, tell him we hydrate as needed.

Midlunch, Michelle brings bread. More Rioja.

I'm a little buzzed when we ask for the check. I figure I'll go downstairs to the market area of the store, look for the vegetable guy I like. He calls me "man." I call him "hey." At Christmas time he phones one of his suppliers, Enzo Ferrari (his real name), to find out when the baby artichokes will come in. "Hey," I say today, "got chard? Got cardone?" He answers: "Right over here, man. Look how beautiful."

We talk about the relative benefits of organic. Does he recommend organic bananas, for example? Does he actually like kale? He smiles and shakes his head no.

Me neither, I say. Another item for the eight plan, if I can learn to like it.

On my way out I make my way to the cracker section. Sweet potato crackers, orange; beet crackers, red. One of each.

7 / You're Not Going to Eat That, Are You?

I'm smarter than squirrels. But not by much.

When they raided my bird feeder, I took action. The feeder hung from one of our apple trees. It looked like a little cabin with top-to-bottom windows on two sides, through which you see the seed. It had a spacious wrap-around porch-perch-platform. The slightest agitation, a blue jay coming in for a landing, a pair of nuthatches shoveling through the mix with their pointer beaks, caused a gentle cascade of seed onto the platform. It was an interdisciplinary seed mix (all birds welcome, something for everyone). A full feeder ought to have lasted a week or so.

But, squirrels.

Whenever I filled the feeder, as soon as I was in the house they climbed face-first down the six feet of the steel cable from the apple tree to the feeder roof, then somersaulted onto platform. It was an impressive gymnastic feat. Then came a pillaging, gorging rampage that cleaned out the stores in an hour or two.

For a while I took potshots at them with a BB gun from an upstairs bedroom.

"I wish you wouldn't do that," my wife said.

"This is my squirrel control program."

"It's terrible. You should be ashamed of yourself."

On one hand, I was just a little ashamed of myself. It was so easy. And, to be honest, kind of fun. But, I admit, it was a perverse kind of fun. On the other hand, I felt like a vigilante, righteous about taking the law into my own hands. What law? The law of nature. Man against creature. I was bending squirrels to my will.

Also the law of the land. I was exercising my constitutional right to bear BB gun and protect my property.

"You kill them," she said.

"I hurt them a little," I said. "But I don't kill them."

I knew for a possible fact that I didn't kill them. When I was eight years old, one autumn evening Harold Rice, two doors down from our house, had raked up a pile of leaves and was burning them in his garden out behind his house. Like most eight-year-olds, I was interested in fire. I wandered into his yard that evening and got close to the fire, which had burned down to a smoldering pile. Thinking I might resuscitate it, I leaned over the fire and began stirring it with a stick, exposing, in that posture, my eight-year-old backside. A kid named Gary Schaffer, who lived in the next house over from the Rices', older than me by a couple years and known, at least by me, to have a mean streak, was lurking in the bushes, armed with a BB gun. He saw my backside as an open invitation, an irresistible target. I took one on the cheek, and it hurt, a lot. But it didn't kill me.

My wife asks now: "How do you know you don't kill them?"

Violence begets violence. Had I become Gary Schaffer, taking my shame, humiliation, and hurt out on innocent creatures?

A squirrel, I was sure, has a tougher hide than a tender eight-year-old boy. I told her I just knew it.

"If they would leave the feeder alone," I said, "we could co-exist."

A friend of ours says he eats squirrel. Or he used to. Raised on a farm in Tennessee, he says his mother made squirrel stew. They were tasty.

"We could eat them," I say to my wife.

"Don't be ridiculous."

"What about Bruce?" I said. "He used to eat them."

"No anymore."

"They probably taste like chicken. Only gamy."

"I hate that word, *gamy*."

"Okay, wild."

"Squirrels are rodents."

I would need to graduate to a deadlier weapon. A pellet gun or a .22. I said so.

"You've never hunted anything. You don't fish. You don't even garden. You go to Kroger."

I hunted frogs as a kid, with the same BB gun I was using now. Killing frogs for sport, mostly, Gary Schaffer–style, though one time Roger Kipfmiller and I, after bagging fifty or so, took them home for his dad to cook up a batch of frog legs. They tasted like chicken.

I remind her I hunted pheasants up north with Steve, my cousin. He let me handle a real shotgun.

"That wasn't hunting. Those birds were planted. And they weren't even pheasants."

They were chukars, a game bird in the partridge family. When the dog flushed them out of the grass I thought they flew as if their heart wasn't really in it, as if they were a little bit drunk. Steve and I and his son blasted away, all three of us at once. They didn't stand a chance.

"One of them was a pheasant," I said. "I'm sure of it." I wasn't sure. Adding: "We eat rabbit. Why not squirrel?"

In addition to being a cute animal, rabbit makes a fine meal, tasting somewhat like chicken, only slightly gamy. But a good rabbit is hard to find where we live. I see them in a gourmet market, at a scandalous price. They are not much in demand. A friend who had an Italian restaurant down the road from us put rabbit on the menu, then took rabbit off the menu. Americans wouldn't order rabbit.

We recently discovered that Norm, our potato and egg man at the Eastern Market, brings a couple frozen rabbits with him every Saturday. Domestic bunnies, they're in the cooler, next to frozen chickens.

My wife and I take turns. Her rabbit recipe, akin to a fricassee, she got from her aunt Teresa in Italy; mine, a roast, I got from Trattoria Mario in Florence.

If rabbit, why not squirrel?

There is a long tradition of squirrel eating in the southern United States. Hence the testimony of Bruce, our Tennessee-born pal. Witness squirrel scholars at the University of Michigan who report that squirrels "have economic importance in some states, such as Mississippi, where 2.5 million are harvested each year with an economic impact of $12.5 million."

At length my wife prevails upon me to lay down arms. During this ceasefire I test bird feeder baffling systems, installing metal guards on the steel cable between the feeder and the apple tree limb. The first device looks like a recycled cymbal from a kid's drum set. It sort of works. Approaching from above, nose-first, a few squirrels reverse course, a delight to watch, and scramble back up the cable; the more determined ones—starved, determined, brazen—bypass the baffle, scare away all the birds, and eat everything. I try another baffle, which is funnel-shaped, reminding me of a metal dunce cap. It's a little more effective. But ultimately, same result: a load of feed disappears in a morning or afternoon. I wonder if squirrels gloat.

It's the idea of some foods, like squirrel, that's downright distasteful. You don't even have to taste beef tongue or heart, for example, to know that you don't like it. Most people I know would just say no to tripe or snails or horse meat. (I had pony ragù in Verona a few years ago—it was delicious.) In China last year we ate fried bugs and fried pig intestine. An acquaintance came home from there having been asked, at a ceremonial function where he was a guest, to eat a toad.

At an all-rabbit banquet one night my wife and I sat across the table from Tony Moraccini, a San Marino guy, a great cook who had supervised the evening's rabbit prep and cooking. His father, Tony said, had slaughtered pigs back in San Marino and Italy, working seven days a week for a few months every fall.

"When I was a kid we ate every piece of pig there was," he said. "Ears, cheeks, feet. The blood was always saved to make pudding."

He said there was only one thing he didn't like and could not eat. Lungs.

Ew.

I read recently that London has a squirrel problem. A public nuisance like the pigeons in Venice, the London squirrel population numbers in the millions. Author and chef Robert Owen Brown, described as "a true hunter-gatherer, a darling, and an all-round good egg," suggests that we just eat the little buggers. In his most recent cookbook, *Crispy Squirrel and Vimto Trifle*, he serves up the how-to. According to Brown, squirrel is "a delicious meat—incredibly sweet and nutty (thanks to its berry and nut-based diet) and very, very lean. The loin is very small so you cook it exactly as you would a rabbit, either very quickly or for a long time."

That's good enough for me. (But not my wife.) Here's the rub: I would have to kill them. Kill. Them. And then of course: head, fur, blood, guts, bone, feet.

I shop at Kroger.

After baffle failure I take down my little house on the apple tree and post a finch feeder on a crook right outside the kitchen window, thinking squirrels will leave it alone. Wrong. For sport, for their own perverse pleasure, the squirrels will not be denied. They shinny up the crook, hug the finch feeder, and attempt to violate it.

A last ditch effort: I grease the crook with Crisco, and by God, it works. The pesky things shinny up eighteen to twenty-four inches and then lose traction, slowly sliding down the greased pole. It's an effective, nonviolent solution. And it's highly entertaining. It's also labor intensive. One coat of Crisco lasts an afternoon. I realize I'll have to factor the cost of lube—in time and money—into bird feeding.

But for just an afternoon, it's enough. I finally feel smarter than a squirrel.

8 / Clean Up Your Act

"I love this thing," I tell my daughter.

I'm washing dishes at her house. My wife and I are staying here while the bathrooms at our place are remodeled. She's home from China for ten days, for our son's wedding.

It's 3:00 a.m.

Her husband and one of the boys are upstairs, sleeping. The little one, still on Shanghai time, a twelve-hour time difference, is wide awake. He's two years old. He's just eaten a plate of eggs. By nature I'm an early bird. I'm keeping them company.

The thing I love, I tell her, is this strainer that lies flat across half her kitchen sink. It looks like a grill. You wash a dish, lay it on the strainer. When you're done, you dry the dishes, put them away, roll up the strainer and put it away.

"Where did it come from?" she asks.

"Mom bought it."

She tells me she thinks washing dishes by hand is gross.

"What do you mean?"

"I mean it's gross. They don't get clean."

The six weeks we've stayed here, I've had something of a conversion experience. It's Zen and the art of washing dishes. I've begun to look forward to the job. Some days I grab a stray glass or coffee cup and wash it just for the sheer joy of placing the rinsed item on the rack.

I hold up a sponge now, show her the soap suds. "Of course they get clean," I say.

She shakes her head, tells me it's disgusting.

"Soap, water, hot rinse," I say. "Put them together and what do you get?"

She shakes her head, points at the dishwasher.

When I was a kid, my mother washed dishes every night after supper. My brother and I took turns drying them. We did not have the benefit of this stylish strainer; from the cabinet under the sink we pulled a clunky old pink, plastic-coated rack that sat on a stiff pink pad that collected drips and drained them into the sink. Washing dishes was a chore. I didn't like it. I carried this animus into adult life and, when I set up housekeeping, fully embraced the dishwasher.

All that has changed.

"They're clean," I insist.

She reaches out, pulls the wet dish towel from my hand, feels it, smells it.

"I'm sorry, Dad," she says. "Dishes should go in the dishwasher. They get sterilized."

Do we need sterile dishes?

The world is crawling, flying, swimming with bad bugs. In the mideighties I read an *Atlantic* article on the poultry industry and Ronald Reagan's administration relaxing regulations. The article was titled "Dirty Chicken." It made an impression. In 2003, in the midst of the SARS scare, products like Purell showed up in the classrooms where I taught. They were everywhere. Elbow bumps replaced handshakes. I adopted the sleeve sneeze. There's never been a retreat, even though there's a robust literature on good bacteria and the perils of being too sanitary.

Around the time I finished high school, hippie culture was in full swing. Nature, the ethos of the time suggested, was good. Nature was also in trouble. We knew something about Dow Chemical and the dioxin floodplain in our backyard.

But the music, the tie-dye and beads, the dope—all that stuff was seductive. With a handful of classmates I walked out of school on the first Earth Day. I said "far out" and flashed the peace sign. (I tried wearing beads but couldn't make it work.) Soon after graduation, my friend Dan Leman (a.k.a. DL) started working for Cliff Compton, a farmer who lived a few miles west of town. Cliff farmed a lot of acres, a lot of nature. Dan drove tractor for him. So did a hippie guy named Wyatt.

That long summer, on warm evenings we drove out to Wyatt's rented house on Carter Road. He lived with a hippie woman named Nell. They were married, I think. They had a little girl who tramped around the dusty driveway in a dress and bare feet and watched with curiosity when her father brought out a hash pipe or rolled joints.

At that time, on the Mothers of Invention's LP *We're Only in It for the Money*, Frank Zappa lampooned this back-to-nature thing in the song "Flower Punk," singing about love-ins and hippies who sit and play their bongos. We knew better than to drink the water in Higgins Lake, but on weekends in the woods up north, no one worried much about a little dirt. Dirt was okay, man.

Near the end of his tenure with Cliff, DL volunteered his services redecorating the Rat Hole Bar, our local basement saloon. The barnwood craze was just getting started. It was a way of bringing nature right into your living room. He nailed a lot of it to the walls in the bar. Also, in a stroke of genius, he repurposed worn out hog-feeding troughs (Cliff also raised hogs), cleaning them up and hanging them, at elbow level, on the walls adjacent to the bar.

Cleaned them up.

Dishwashers, I think, were not yet in widespread use in my hometown. Nor were power washers. The troughs did not smell. I'm pretty sure they had not been sterilized. If you thought about it, the hog trough idea seemed both clever and disgusting. Nobody thought about it.

"Don't get me wrong," my daughter says. "The rack is cool. But instead of putting the dishes away, why don't you just load them into the dishwasher?"

"I guess I could." But what about the Zen? Somehow I can't square the dishwasher with my Zen.

"It's what you do at your house," she says.

She's right. The vigorous rinse. I've been told not to do that, not to wash the dishes before they go in the dishwasher, not to rinse the dishes at all before they go in the dishwasher. Those food particles remaining on bowls and plates, the argument goes, mix with the dish detergent and water and become a powerful cleaning agent. A whirling slurry of garbage gets your dishes clean. Even scuds the dried egg yolk off the two-year-old's plate.

One night, a few days after they've gone back to China, still at our daughter's house, I'm stepping into the shower. My wife tells me where the shower soap is.

I tell I don't need soap.

"You don't use soap?"

"I do not."

"Not ever?"

"Somewhere between rarely and never."

"And you don't feel dirty?"

I tell her I get clean. Clean as an American Indian standing in a stream in the land of sky-blue water. Do you suppose they used soap? Did they keep a bar of Irish Spring or Dove in the tepee, lather up and rinse off down at the creek?

"Soap is bad for you," I say.

She tells me I'm crazy.

We each have our zones of purity.

9 / Alien Pleasures

This morning at 5:00 a.m., when I sit down next to her on the couch and hand her a cappuccino, my wife detects something foul on my breath.

She takes the coffee, turns her head, and gently pushes me away. "What did you eat?"

We stayed with the grandchildren last night at our daughter's house, while she and her husband went out. Later today I'm driving up to visit the county clerk for marriage and birth certificates. Our daughter is making a request for citizenship in San Marino, for her kids and for herself.

"A leftover hot dog," I say. "I couldn't help myself."

I noticed it last night, just before we went to bed, resting on the cutting board next to the cooktop. It was dark, leathery, deep reddish brown, just on the verge of cracking open. A leftover hot dog that must have been cooked for the two future citizens, the five-year-old or the two-year-old. A leftover hot dog, unwanted by small children. This morning it was cold, the fats inside it congealed, its leathery skin even leatherier. The minute I saw it the night before, I wanted that hot dog. There was about it a certain air of inevitability.

Fresh out of bed this morning I ate it cold, in five bites.

I expect my wife will say, "*che schifo*." Italian for "That's disgusting." Reverso Dictionary, a translation site I just discovered, also suggests "it sucks," "it stinks," "it blows," "it's gross," "it's crap," "it's garbage." You get the idea.

It was delicious.

There are, of course, luscious leftovers that are inviting in the morning. Foods, for example, that are better the next day. Stews, a boiled or roasted potato, a stalk of mushy broccoli, even cold pasta. Perhaps best, even better than leftover hot dog, is cold pizza.

According the Delish, a website that reports on food news and food trends, 53 percent of Americans polled said they prefer cold pizza to traditional breakfast foods in the morning. Not pizza. *Cold* pizza. That's definitely me. What a pleasure it is to come downstairs in the morning, finding the thin square cardboard box on the kitchen counter, its lid slightly ajar, and inside it two to three cold slices, the cheese just beginning to harden, the sauce cooled; and the crust beneath the cheese and sauce a little bit sodden, still tough around the edges.

If I had waited, if I had asked them, I've pretty sure neither of my grandsons would have wanted to eat that cold hot dog. Cold hot dog, like cold pizza, is big people food.

Big American people food.

For some reason, the Republic of San Marino has recently decided it wants more citizens. This after a long history of regulations limiting who can become a citizen. The criteria were based strictly on parentage and gender. In marriage a San Marino citizen could confer citizenship on his non-Sammarinese spouse and eventual offspring.

Not his or *her* spouse, not his or *her* offspring.

Only male citizens enjoyed the prerogative of marrying an alien and making their wives and kids official.

It was a policy based on residual—or, rather, historic—sexism. There were practical reasons. San Marino is a small country—twenty-four square miles, population thirty-three thousand. There's only so much room. And there are definitely cultural integrity issues at play. The country does not see itself as a melting pot or tossed salad. Though why the spouses and children of women Sammarinese would sully the culture more than those of men is not exactly clear. We would have to ask the men in power to explain that.

Over time I have come to question the idea of dual citizenship, maybe because I am on the outs. I am, after all, a male alien. No RSM citizenship for me. But really: Can one be faithful to two countries any more than he can be faithful to two wives?

Then again, the government does leave the door open, if just a crack. If I took up residency in San Marino today, after thirty years, at which point I would be ninety-seven years old, I could request citizenship. My case would be brought before the grand and general counsel for review. Background checks would probably be required, in a search for criminal behavior and character traits that might be seen as a potential pollutant of pure San Marino culture.

"This suitor," one grand counselor would say to the next, having reviewed my dossier, "eats leftover hot dogs for breakfast."

To which the general response would be: "*Che schifo!*"

And then: citizenship denied.

That term, *schifo*, has always struck me as powerful, viscerally expressive in the extreme, carrying the same impact as *fuck* or *shit* in English, maybe because *schifo* is often said with a distinctly shriveling look, in an attitude of total disgust and revulsion.

Given its power, I thought it might be a dialect term. But come to find out *schifo* is a standard Italian term (from *schifare*, a verb meaning "to disgust"), its usage extending as far back as Boccaccio and Petrarch, to the very beginning of the Italian language. Evidently, unlike *shit*, you can say *schifo* in front of anyone in Italy without giving offense.

Or not. To disapprove of what someone eats, what someone relishes, to refer to it as a *schifenza*, is offensive.

Early in our marriage, having spent a night with her relatives down the coast from San Marino, I came down stairs one morning, possibly mildly hungover, to the smell of fish broth cooking. Its stench permeated the house.

"It's good," my wife said.

The word *miasma* came to my mind. "If you say so," I said.

She said that she loved it, that I really needed to try it.

"Che schifo," I said. I was new to the language and thought I would try out the expression. To which she took grave offense. When someone insults what you love, it's hard to be cool.

One of her relatives used to make a special cake around Easter, called *pagnotta di Pasqua*. Its near relative was *pagnotta romagnola*, a cake made with honey, sugar, raisins, and anisette, a sweet, fragrant breakfast or dessert food. My father-in-law made one, studiously perfecting the recipe in his retirement. For me it was love at first bite.

This old aunt's *pagnotta di Pasqua* was not *romagnola*. She was from Fano, in the Marches region. (Nearby residents, instead of telling someone to go to hell, tell them to go to Fano.) She added grated cheese to the recipe, which is evidently what they do in Fano, but which was nothing less than a grotesque mistake. If there was honey, sugar, raisins, and anisette in her pagnotta, you couldn't tell. All you could taste was cheese. It was an olfactory offense, a gustatory disaster.

Everyone in our family agreed, *La pagnotta della zia Iride fa schifo.* Aunt Iris's *pagnotta* is disgusting. Everyone, that is, except a cousin who grew up eating it.

I was delighted to discover that from *schifo*, in English we get the slangy and very pungent *skeevy*. Urban Dictionary provides this definition—Shifty, sleazy, creepy, dirty, dodgy, nasty—and offers these delicious examples of how the word is used:

> Have you seen Britney Spears' latest husband? Ugh, he's so skeevy.
>
> Eeeew, look at that skeevy guy over there with the white plastic shoes.
>
> Of course there's no guarantee. He bought the thing from some skeevy dude in an alley.

Just as I can recall my first whiff of fish broth, I can pinpoint my first skeevy contact with the word, in Steely Dan's "Cousin Dupree," a song about a lecherous guy with a skeevy look in his eyes. Like scummy and scuzzy and scruffy, skeevy conveys disgust and revulsion, coming into English, according to Merriam-Webster, by way of New York and New Jersey Italians and their use of *schifo*.

"Do you work for a funeral home?"

Post-coffee, post-cold-hot-dog, I'm standing at the cashier's window at the county clerk's office. You order your documents, then pay while they're being printed and stamped with the official raised seal. The cashier has a spray of brown hair tied up on top of her head and an easy smile.

I tell her no one has ever asked me that question.

"Sorry," she says.

I hand her my credit card. "Don't be sorry," I say. "I liked it."

"Usually," she says, "a person gets just one certificate. Not a bunch of them." She adds, apropos of something, "Funeral directors are some of the best dressed people who come in here."

She looks a lot younger than the rest of the women working in records (by the looks of it, it's an all-women operation).

"Spiffy," I say. "Like insurance salesmen."

She gives me a fishy look.

"You know what *spiffy* means."

"Well put together," she says.

I make a mental note: look up the origins of *spiffy*, which must be the antithesis of skeevy. (Probably from British English "spiff," referring in 1853 to a well-dressed man, though "spiflicated drunk," American usage first noted in 1902, carries a skeevy connotation.)

Behind me is a guy paying for a concealed weapon permit. I turn and nod. He's much better put together this morning than I am.

With hot dog on my breath, I figure I'm somewhere between spiffy and skeevy. And I'm perfectly all right with that.

10 / Ecumenical Meat Loaf

What got my attention was a BuzzFeed post I saw a few days ago. I would put it in the snarky-remarks-Europeans-make-about-Americans category.

Lots of snark. So much you need subcategories. In this case, the issue was what irritates Europeans about Americans who travel abroad. For example: Americans talk too loud, Americans tell what state they come from (people from Michigan, raise your hand). Americans are polite, they smile all the time, they engage total strangers, like cashiers, in conversation. They are fastidious about finding trashcans. They require lots of ice.

Somehow I had found my way to the food category and the twenty-six questions about food that non-Americans want answered. Do Americans eat glazed doughnuts for breakfast? Do Americans eat spaghetti out of a can? Do they eat grilled cheese with ketchup? Do they eat peanut butter out of the jar with a spoon?

Do they eat cold pizza?

Hell yes.

Do they really eat meat loaf? WTF is that?

Excuse me? WTF is what? Meat loaf?

Okay, American food culture—there are issues. In my final twenty-five years of teaching, I regularly invited students to talk about what they ate for dinner. I admit, what I heard did not sound appetizing. For the most part their diets were dominated by industrial, preservative-enhanced, microwave-ready pseudo-foods. A popular breakfast of champions to carry into the classroom was an Otis Spunkmeyer Chocolate Chunk Cookie (chunk not chip) and a twenty-ounce Mountain Dew. Or a caramel Frappuccino with a bag of chips. Or cold Pop-Tarts and vitaminwater.

So much ready-to-eat garbage. I had not thought junk could sustain so many.

But meat loaf? WTF? Really?

I grew up eating meat loaf. When I was nine my mother's was the ideal meat loaf, which stands to reason. A kid's benchmarks are always a work in progress.

Her meat loaf was a ground beef, bread crumb, and egg mix, seasoned with salt and pepper, the only spices she made use of. There also might have been something greenish added. And I have to suspect, somewhere in the mix was a dollop of cream of mushroom soup. This mound of meat, mixed and massaged, went into the bread pan she also used for pumpkin and banana breads. The pan ensured its loafness. What came out was brown, moist, and flavorful. Sliced, I do not think we put ketchup on it. And I have no recollection of meat loaf sandwiches, meaning we must have eaten all of it in one sitting.

Benchmarks. A work in progress. A life in meat loafs. Some of them dubious.

Shortly after graduating from high school I ate lunch at a friend's house. He was nineteen and married, his wife eighteen and pregnant. He served a meat loaf that had a distinctive flavor. The acronym was not in use or part of our lexicon yet, but I remember thinking: WTF. Breakfast sausage, he said. It was part of the mix. I took another bite. Distinctive, though not altogether felicitous.

A few years later, finding myself twenty-five and married, my wife not yet pregnant, I tried to recreate my mother's meat loaf. I succeeded, but found myself wondering, What is success? There followed decades of meat loaf, in diners and bars, in egg joints, in roadside Eat-at-Joe's, meat loafs with mushrooms piled on top, meat loafs slathered with barbecue sauce; also, so many meat loafs writ small; I mean Swedish meatballs in church basements (and not a Swede in sight), spag and balls washed down with beer, meatball sandwiches glistening with runny spicy red tomato glop.

Then came revelation: At my mother-in-law's table, *polpette*, meatballs that she somewhat grudgingly cooked and that my wife and I could not eat fast enough. Grudgingly because, as a kid in Italy between world wars, the daughter of a man who worked for a butcher and brought home lots of meat scraps, my mother-in-law had eaten way too many meatballs and, as a result, had grown to hate them.

A quick examination of the historical record suggests that, whether meatball or meat loaf, mini or maxi, short form or long form, meat loaf is an ecumenical food, casting a long shadow, as *Bon Appétit* attests: "There are competing histories, including the belief that meat loaf, or its closest antecedent, emerged in medieval Europe, around the fifth century, in a Mediterranean dish of finely diced meat scraps joined with fruits, nuts and seasonings." In *What's Cooking America*, ground meat is traced back as far as Genghis Khan. In the thirteenth century, GK and the Golden Horde "softened the meat by placing [patties] under the saddles of their horses while riding into battle. When it was time to eat, the meat would be eaten raw, having been tenderized by the saddle and the back of the horse." In addition to horse, I think I smell *kafta*, a signature food in Middle Eastern cuisine, essentially meat loaf on a stick.

Meat loaf is a source of nutrition and joy in so many countries: Argentina has *pan de carne*; Austria, *Faschierter Braten*; Belgium, *veles brood*; Chile, *asado alemán*; Cuba, *pulpeta*; Denmark, *foreloren hare*; Germany, *Hackbraten*; Poland, *pieczeń rzymska*; Sweden, *köttfärslimpa*; Turkey, *dalyan köfte*.

Did I mention *polpette*?

Outside our building in San Marino one day I chat up Mr. Riccardi, who lives in the apartment immediately below ours.

From both apartments there is a full view of Mount Titano in San Marino. Originally from Genova, Mr. Riccardi is a retired financial manager. He rides a motorcycle. He and his wife take Italy vacations in their motorhome. Walking down the interior stairway of the building, I frequently smell good food being prepared in their apartment. Into this apartment some years ago, after a pipe in our apartment burst, a stream of our water flowed, requiring repairs, theirs and ours.

In the stairway and outside on the sidewalk, I've worked on repairing this relationship.

"Where do you eat," I ask him this day, "when you go out to a restaurant around here?"

He paused to think, smiled and nodded, then named a number of places, all within the confines of little San Marino, all within a short driving distance: 5 Vie in Falciano, Il Ghetto da Ottavio in San Marino Città, Osteria da Burinon in Cailungo, Osteria Unione in Acquaviva.

We try them all. We drive up toward Mount Titano and hook right, descending the mountain toward Acquaviva. At Osteria Unione we meet Lidia, proprietor and chief cook, who serves real local home cooking. At our first visit, for lunch she serves polpettone, meatball writ large, which is to say meat loaf. It is a life-changing experience, a meat loaf for the gods, made with the beef she has boiled to make broth, then extracted, chopped, and mixed with bread crumbs, egg, parsley, garlic, and Parmigiano-Reggiano.

Back home I made Lidia's meat loaf once a week until my wife and kids said stop, enough already. My reaction was, WTF? Is there a better food?

No, there is not.

Do Americans really eat meat loaf? Yes, they do.

Doesn't everyone?

11 / Good Eggs

"I think these eggs have been fertilized," my wife says.

I'm spreading correct peanut butter on a piece of toast. That's peanut butter minus all the ingredients that make peanut butter taste good (salt, sugar, hydrogenated oils, mono- and diglycerides); peanut butter in its purest, oiliest, sludgiest, and least manageable state.

"Fertilized?"

Two scrambled eggs every morning. I cook them for her in a little olive oil, with a light sprinkling of salt. She likes her eggs wet, a preference I have always questioned and which she has always maintained is perfectly safe. When she was a kid back in Italy, her grandmother made her drink a raw egg some mornings. It doesn't get much wetter than that. She doesn't say she liked it; what she seems is *proud* of it. She drank her egg down while her sister threw hers up. Not because there was anything wrong with the egg, my wife says. I think: Maybe because there was something right with her sister.

I wonder what a fertilized egg would taste like.

Some years ago, long before I converted to "real" peanut butter, I caved on industrial eggs. Up to then I bought a dozen white ones in the squeaky white Styrofoam cartons, bought them wherever I found them, grocery stores, party stores, gas stations, with total confidence in what was inside. Then eggs became suspect, full of cholesterol, and the industrial egg, in particular, like everything Big Food touches, was especially corrupt.

These days I buy eggs that are supposed to be virtuous. They're brown. They come in cardboard cartons made from recycled paper. The package says "free range," "no antibiotics," "no hormones." I can't assess the difference in taste or yolk density. To me, they taste like eggs, just like the other ones did. Some mornings there's the shock of double yolks. It's a reminder of the creature potential in eggs—eventual feathers, beaks, feet.

She holds up her plate now for me to taste the fertilized egg.

I smell them—there's definitely a funny ammonia thing going on—and try a bite.

"Tastes like feet," I say, and dump the eggs in the sink.

"Too bad," she says. "They were very red."

My wife has long maintained the eggs in Italy are better than the ones in the United States. Not just different. Better. She points to the yolk as evidence, the *rosso dell'uovo*, the red of the egg, as the Italians call it. And she is right about one thing. Egg yolks in Italy are different, a brighter, deeper yellow. You see it when you break an egg in a pan. You see it when you roll tagliatelle onto your fork. Cruising the pasta section of a grocery store in the United States, you can tell the American-made pasta. It has a pale, bleached color. Next to it on the shelf, a pasta imported from Italy, especially the artisanal stuff, is bright yellow, almost too bright to be believed.

Nobody I know in Italy eats eggs for breakfast. But you see eggs on the menu, gorgeous blazing yellow frittatas, dishes of scrambled eggs during truffle season. Go out for truffles in the fall, typically at the outset of the meal they shave truffle onto eggs. You eat these eggs and marvel that something could be so good.

A few years ago we were in Acqualagna, a hill town north of Assisi, having a truffle lunch. When they brought out the eggs, one of our friends scowled and shook her head.

"What is it?" I asked.

"The eggs," she said. "They give the chickens medicine to color the eggs."

"Medicine?"

"Yes, you know, chemicals to make the yolks redder. Just look at them."

"You're not going to eat them?"

"No."

The eggs looked beautiful, preternaturally yellow, worthy of the big fat truffle the server was holding. At the table, there seemed to be general disagreement with her. The eggs were fine. The yolks were naturally "red." Get over it. I got over it, over a plate of those eggs, picturing pill-popping hens hopped up on . . . something.

A few years after that, our daughter, fresh out of culinary school, stayed over in Italy a couple months, learning at the cousins' trattoria to make pasta by hand: hand-mixed, hand-rolled dough; hand-cut tagliatelle. One morning she made an offhand comment about the eggs, their color, how "red" they were.

"It's what they put in the feed," my wife's cousin Marina said.

Wait, what?

"What the chickens eat makes the yolks that color."

So . . . medicine?

In Italy, as in the United States, there are eggs, and there are eggs.

I recall my shock, standing in the *supermercato* one day in San Marino. I had gone to buy a dozen eggs. Where do you look? I headed for the refrigerated cases, finding cheeses and dairy, but no eggs. "Over there," I was told when I finally asked someone. What? In the middle of the store, on pallets, eggs packaged by the half dozen, sitting there at room temperature.

I bought my half dozen, took them home, and dutifully put them in the fridge.

In the United States, by law, eggs are washed and refrigerated within thirty-six hours of the time they are laid and collected. They remain refrigerated through packaging, distribution, stocking in stores, right up to the point of sale (and after). According to the American Egg Board, yearly egg production in the United States is staggering: seventy-nine billion eggs a year. According to the board, that's 285 million "layers" coming to work every day, sitting around doing what comes natural to them. Sixty-two companies provide 85 percent of U.S. production, many of those companies with a million hens; sixteen of those companies with more than five million hens each. If you have a weak stomach, don't look too closely at the egg industry.

Washing and chilling is how U.S. producers address the salmonella problem. The European model is different. In general, European producers are more hen-friendly. There's a little more space, more room for hens to roost. Eggs going to market remain at room temperature, unwashed. The "cuticle," a parting gift of hens to eggs, is a coating that protects the egg from disease. Unwashed eggs keep their cuticle.

How safe are eggs anywhere?

The USDA says, "There are no significant differences affecting health between organic and conventional eggs."

But who's going to believe them?

It's hard to trust your food, just as it's hard to trust your news. According to *World Poultry*, "In Europe alone over 100,000 cases [of salmonella] are reported each year and in the United States there are approximately 40,000 cases reported annually. Since many milder cases are not diagnosed or reported, the actual number of infections may be over thirty times higher." (Thirty times higher?) Makes me glad the United States requires egg wash. Then there's this, from *Food Safety News*: "Salmonella bacteria causes about 1.2 *million* foodborne illnesses in the U.S. annually, according to the Centers for Disease Control and Prevention. The microorganism causes about 450 deaths every year." Evidently there are a lot of bad eggs out there. Unfortunately, they all look about the same.

But what about those virtuous eggs I've been buying? "Cage free" means during recess a hen might get to scratch a patch of ground the size of a postage stamp, and probably not even every day. Most of the hens are "debeaked," a practice almost too brutal and offensive to imagine, which is done to reduce cannibalism. A National Public Radio story on eggs shoots down the "no antibiotics" and "no hormones" claims. Antibiotics are rarely used in U.S. egg production. So that disclaimer is meaningless.

And hormones? "It's illegal to give hormones to poultry, and no large-scale farms in the U.S. do so." So those no-antibiotics and no-hormones labels are about like a "contains no cholesterol" claim on bottled water.

The best eggs in the United States these days, brought to market under the most natural and humane circumstances, are pastured eggs. How much are you willing to spend? How much do you value purity and safety in your food? How real is risk? How elastic are your ethics?

In the end, maybe we want to eat what we've always loved. I may have gone natural, but I still dream about Jif peanut butter. When our kids were small, my mother-in-law would whip up *uovo sbattuto* for them. Sometimes in the morning to give them a proper launch, or in the afternoon for snack (*merenda*), or at the end of a meal for dessert, she beat sugar into raw egg yolk and spooned it into their mouths. They loved it. In an online forum dedicated to questions of child-rearing in Italy, a mother swears by raw egg and sugar. She reports: "I miei lo mangiano tutti i giorni la mattina, e non prendono mai il raffredore." (My children have one every morning. They never catch a cold.)

Let there be eggs. Let them be yellow, red, green, or blue.

Fertilized? It turns out, like many things egg-related, it's difficult to taste the difference. Nevertheless, it's not hard to foresee a new disclaimer on egg cartons: "Cage free, no hormones, no antibiotics. Extra-virgin hens."

12 / *Bombolone*, Venus, Boar

In Italian, the sin of gluttony is *gola*. *Golosità*.

In Italy, it's so easy to be *goloso*.

I'm thinking about gluttony the day my wife and I drive to Urbino. From Pesaro it's a forty-kilometer drive I do not love, on a two-lane road through village after village, past Montelabbate and Colbordolo, past Gallo and Morcia. Every few kilometers you have to brake for a roundabout. You get stuck behind trucks and vans, behind decrepit Fiats driven by old men. Then around Trasanni, five to ten kilometers from Urbino, the road straightens out, and the hills rise gloriously, so glorious you almost think you might slow down, pull over, and take in the view.

We don't. We are on a mission.

We've made a special point of arriving in Urbino early today so my wife can have a *bombolone*. She says the Urbino *bombolone* is her favorite (her current favorite), the one she gets at the top of Via Raffaello, at Pasticceria Cartolari.

A *bombolone* is a tube of fried dough, filled with pastry cream, then rolled in sugar. Nobody in their right mind, nobody, that is, but a *golosa*, would eat one. They're heavy, sweet, fattening, and above all they are filling. You need to eat one early in the day. If you come late, Cartolari might have already sold them all. If you're late but not too late, a *bombolone* will cancel your desire for lunch. Nobody in their right mind wants that.

We've come to Urbino for *bomboloni* and to see the Ducal Palace, where Titian's Venus of Urbino is on loan from the Uffizi. We've come, also, just to be in Urbino. Storybook city. Medieval city on a hill. City of cobblestone stairways that tunnel into side streets with the look of dark alleys, down and up which you can be briefly and delightfully lost.

We are goloso for this place.

Full of *bomboloni*, studiously *before* visiting Venus, we stagger down Via Raffaello, the steepest street in Urbino, past Raffaello's house, and into the main piazza where university students, fresh from their dissertation defenses, wear their laurels and parade with family and friends up and down the streets.

While my wife steps into a ceramic shop, I have another coffee and make inquiries about lunch.

"Due Leone?" I ask the bartender.

"No lunch," he says. "They serve only dinner on weekdays."

"Otherwise?"

"La Fornarina."

I tell him we've been here. We walked by it just now. The special today is stewed boar, polenta, and baked apple. Tempting. But I'd like to try something new.

He fetches a placemat with a map on it; a placemap. "Al Cantuccio," he says. He makes a dot on the map, slides it across the bar in front of me.

I'm pretty sure I can find this dot.

I walk up in the direction of the Ducal Palace and take an alley to the left. From a palazzo window along the way comes the sound of piano, a music student practicing. Further on, more practicing, a violin, a French horn. The street bends slightly to the left, slopes down, and stops abruptly at the edge of the hill town.

Across the way, a few kilometers off, are those hills we saw driving in. To the left, just around the corner, is Al Cantuccio. I check the menu, peek through the window, check the menu again. Maybe not.

Today at the Ducal Palace the rooms are full of school children, standing in front of paintings, while docents try to hold forth above the din. Here is *Citta' ideale* (the ideal city) by Piero della Francesca. And here is the *Miracle of the Desecrated Host* by Paolo Uccello. And here is *The Mute* by Raffaello. We try to stay a few rooms ahead of the children, stopping in Federico da Montefeltro's bedroom, in the palace's great hall of tapestries, and in the duke's *studiolo*, the "little study," which includes miracles of inlaid wood, trompe-l'oeil representations of books, candle, hourglass, astrolabe, armor. They are astonishing.

Just as we reach the room with Titian's Venus, not one but two groups of kids arrive and surge toward the painting. The decibel level rises and falls. Venus—there is a lot of her—meets every gaze in the room. The docent draws the children's attention to the roses in her hand; they should associate roses, she says, with the goddess Venus. The docent draws their attention to the two ladies in waiting in the painting's background, rummaging through a chest; the children should associate these women with wedding preparations. The docent draws their attention to the dog, a symbol of fidelity. The painting, she says, is an allegory of marriage. Though there are other interpretations.

Venus, totally exposed and totally at her ease, meets every gaze, unashamed.

"Let's go," my wife says, hooking an arm through mine. She means lunch.

I tell her another visit—I mean another day, another month, another year from now—I would spend more time in the *studiolo*.

For lunch, we decide to go with what we know. At La Fornarina the boar is stewed with onion, carrot, celery. Also bay leaves and juniper berries. We have half a liter of the house wine. It's enough. The polenta is firm and holds the boar sauce. The berries pop in your mouth, giving off a piney, ginny flavor.

"What do you think," I ask, setting down my fork. "Dessert?"

The waiter brings us one *torta della nonna*, which has a lemon custard, and a few slices of *crostata*, a standard pastry of the region, made with a local *marmellata*.

We walk back up the hill, past Raffaello's house, past Cartolari. No, we couldn't possibly.

On the drive back to Pesaro, and then San Marino, my wife dozes. I enjoy the hills, take it easy around the roundabouts. Who cares if we have to take it slow? *Bombolone*, Venus, boar—it was a very good day.

And the study. Don't forget the study.

Urbino, we'll be back.

13 / Speak to Me

I heard it said once, if you want to learn a foreign language, you have to get a lover.

There is some truth to this. In short order, you might pick up a few stock phrases from said lover, gumdrops such as "You are my everything," "At last we have found each other," "We live but once." It's a start. You listen, you experiment, you flub a lot. You make a little progress. Over time the phrases pile up and spill over, as new, more specific ones are added: "Pick up your socks, please." "The car is making a funny noise." "Are you going to eat that potato?"

Also helpful in foreign language learning are old women and small children. Both frequently repeat themselves without being asked, which comes in handy, and if you're lucky, both speak slowly and enunciate clearly.

Finally, in addition to help from my wife and old women and small children, I have found lady books to be indispensable. I don't know how I could have learned Italian without them.

My mother-in-law left us a substantial library of lady books, works of fiction with titles like *Un certo sorriso* (A certain smile), *Il re della seduzione* (The king of seduction), *Una perduta melodia* (A lost song), *L'avventura più bella* (A most beautiful adventure), *Torna a casa Valeria* (Valery comes home). One of my favorites, the one that really launched me into lady book reading, is *Sotto la neve amore* (Love beneath the snow).

There are so many reasons to read a lady book. To begin with, the language is straightforward. I tried newspapers. Newspapers in Italy are hard for a beginner to read. The grammar is tangled;

the vocabulary is frequently specialized. The legislature did what? A comparative study of readability published in *Reading Research Quarterly* concluded that Italian newspapers score 25 percent higher on a readability scale (meaning more difficult to read) than those written in English. So, it's not just me.

In a good lady book, the authors keep things simple. The stories are loaded with dialogue, which is slowed . . . down . . . conversation. In real time, in real life, at the dinner table or in a bar, chat blows past you. You can't listen fast enough. If you want to learn to gab, it helps to read a lady book. To be sure, there may be a smattering of specialized vocabulary. You might need it. International banking? After reading *Sybil vuole vincere* (Sybil wants to win), I think I might be able to do that job. Then there's plot. Can Dotoressa Maren Harvey complete her research on malaria in the jungles of New Guinea for the London Hospital of Infectious Diseases? Will Nicholas Calder, standing in for her advisor, Professor Russell Brent, agree to guide her in the jungle? You know she will. Because you know he will. They'll be dodging snakes and peeling leeches off each other before you know it. After that, anything can happen. And it does. Throughout these texts there is the language of love, lots of it, which is why you want to learn Italian in the first place.

I married into an all-Italian all-the-time family. After a few months of elbowing my wife at the dinner table and whispering, What did he say? What's so funny? I decided I needed to learn.

We were setting the table for dinner one night at her parents' house.

"I'm totally out of it," I said. "You need to teach me." It seemed like everyone was having so much fun.

My wife held up a stainless steel coaster, like a priest blessing the host, and said, "*Sottobicchiere.*"

"What?"

"*Sottobicchiere.* It's the thing you put under a glass to keep—"

"Right," I said. "I see what it is." I tried saying the word.

"You have to pronounce both *t*'s."

"Are there two *t*'s?" I didn't hear two *t*'s. You couldn't see two *t*'s. I asked her to say it again.

"Sot-to. Sot-to. *Sottobicchiere*. You hear that? Two *t*'s."

I said the word, imperfectly, wondering when in the days and months ahead I was going to need to say *sottobicchiere*, which is a big problem with foreign language learning. What do you need to know? And when do you need to know it?

I told her *sottobicchiere* didn't seem very useful.

She shrugged and said, "It's a start."

I was reminded of trying to learn French, screwing up my mouth and extruding the exotic *u* sound through pursed lips, trying to find enough phlegm in the back of my throat to approximate the *r* sound. From my one French class, I remember only, "Ou est la bibliotheque?" Where is the library? I spent a little time in Paris a few years ago and never found myself in a situation where I needed to ask for the library. Not once.

Sottobicchiere.

Word by word, lady book by lady book, I learned. Thanks to lady books I can now participate in some conversations. Old ladies and children are my preferred interlocutors.

Then there's men.

In Italy you see them in the coffee bars, four or five or six around a table, directing their attention to pink sports gazettes open on the table in front of them (why pink I do not know), or to the television mounted on the wall. You see them and you hear them.

Americano! the men in the local bar yell at me, pointing at the sports gazette. They ask me a question. I know it has something to do with soccer. Do I like it? Drawing on one of my lady books, I could say something like:

My heart swells and beats faster as our time draws near.

Americano! they yell at me, asking me a question about a recent motorcycle race. I have a ready response:

In the depths of my soul I knew the answer was yes, yes yes.

Americano! they yell. This time it's Formula Uno. It sounds like they want to know who my favorite driver is.

A dark-haired fellow with a sensual mouth and smoky eyes.

Fortunately I can shrug my shoulders in Italian. It suffices for them.

Not for me.

In *Hunger of Memory*, Richard Rodriguez reacts to the language of a group of Black teenagers he hears on a bus. The sound of Black dialect, he writes, is the sound of outsiders: "They annoy me for being loud—so self-sufficient and unconcerned by my presence." Like their African American counterparts Rodriguez speaks of, the Italian men I hear speak dialect. They speak it, they live it. They exult in it. It defines who they are. Rodriguez says, "Listening to their shouted laughter, I realize my own quiet . . . Their voices enclose my isolation. I feel envious, envious of their brazen intimacy."

It is an isolation that can't be bridged.

The men in the bar are not outsiders. I am the outsider. I will never feel the connection they feel, mediated by their shared lingo, any more than I will ever feel the shared intimacy of African American kids, mediated by their talk. "They seem glamorous," Rodriguez says. Do they ever.

My wife and I were walking along the sea in Rimini recently, past a restaurant called Lo Squero.

"What's 'lo squero'" she says.

She's asking me?

When we get home I look it up. Boat launch. It sounds like a cool place to hang out, maybe get to know some old ladies and little kids and chat them up. It also sounds like it could be a great setting for a lady book. *James Hancock had just put his sailboat in the water, a forty-six-foot ketch. He was preparing to set sail for Crete. Just then, a pretty blonde astrophysicist named Lucy Worthington approached him. "Looking for a deckhand?" she wondered.*

Sure. Why not?

At last they find each other. And the talk and the love begin.

These days I'm reading Italian crime fiction. I've gotten to know a number of detectives—Antonio Manzini's Rocco Schiavone, Gianrico Carofiglio's Guido Guerieri, Marco Vichi's Commissario Bordelli—guys with the cool of Maximum Bob, in books with the stylistic flavor that calls to mind American writers like Elmore Leonard, Ross Macdonald, and Stephen Dobyns. I haven't been in a situation yet where I needed to ask, "Where'd they find the body?" Nor have I needed to ask, in Italian, "Where is the library?" Bookstore yes; library no. Something tells me in this lifetime I will never get to Dante, a writer who remains as difficult as Chaucer.

For the record, I have, on a number of occasions, used the word *sottobicchiere*, pronouncing both *t*'s. So yes, a lover, old women and children, and lady books. But the greatest of these is the lover.

14 / Do the Work

This morning I reset my Kindle to address a memory issue. I went nuclear and used the factory reset option. That erases everything on the device.

I like the idea of a full erase. To me, wide-open unused space is desirable, especially on a hard drive. Maybe it's the American in me—the lure of the open range and the frontier. It also appeals to the minimalist in me. My sock drawer is more than half empty. I like it that way. How many pairs of socks do I need?

On the other hand, erasing books? Think about your bookshelves. Ours groan under the weight of the books we read last year, and the year before, and the year before that, going way back in time. Your books form you, become a part of you. Picture those shelves completely empty. A little dust, a few stray bookmarks and receipts. Nothing else. It's like mind erase. I've seen dementia. It looks like that.

While I'm fixing my Kindle—at least I hope I'm fixing it—my wife sits across the table from me reading the morning paper (reading the morning iPad). We've had our minimalist breakfast, egg and crunchy dry whole grain toast.

She says, without looking up, "According to this, the human bite changed over time. From an edge-to-edge bite to an overbite." She fixes her mouth, shows me first one bite, then the other. "If hadn't been for overbite, we couldn't pronounce the letter f or v."

I'm only half listening.

"*Smithsonian Magazine*." She shows me her screen, insists I look. "They're called labiodental sounds." She points at her mouth, then touches her bottom lip to her top row of teeth, practices saying *f* words, *v* words.

In front of me, on the table, Kindle. A light tap on Reset is all it takes. Five years of reading, gone.

"Fava," she says. "Vivacious."

I wonder out loud if Arabs have *f* words. Or Eskimos.

"Forest. Figs. Filigree."

Settings, Option, Reset. With a gentle tap, the screen goes dark. Taking a sip of coffee, I watch and wait. The kitchen still smells like toast.

"Falafel," I say.

The reboot starts. This will take Kindle a few minutes.

For a week or so I've been working my way through a novel by Marco Vichi, called *Per nessun motivo* (For no reason), on my Kindle. It's about a guy in his sixties who learns he has a daughter from a love affair in Paris thirty years ago, before he met his wife, before he settled down to become a rich industrialist in Tuscany. His wife discovers an old undelivered letter from the woman in Paris, informing him that he has a daughter. Undelivered because his wife opened the letter thirty years ago and then hid it from him. For whatever reason, she gives him the letter now. That's chapter one.

His name is Antonio. He decides he has to make things right. He goes to Paris, searches for the daughter's mother, his former lover, who turns out to be dead, and for his daughter, who is alive and well, a philosophy student who also works in a real estate office. He arranges to meet her, assuming an alias to hide his identity, and the story unfolds. Should he tell her who he is? Will telling her harm or help her? Will she love him or hate him? The letter, the alias, the dissembling—it's all kind of Shakespearean, with an Italian accent.

The nice thing about reading in a foreign language on a Kindle is the "translation" function. Touch a word, the translation pops up. Another nice thing is that Kindle remembers the words you looked up, stores them in its memory, and will show them to you in list form or play them back on flash cards for vocab drills. *Sobbalzare*, for example. To start, jump, jerk.

My Italian is pretty good, but I'm also a pretty touchy reader. In the five years I've been reading Italian novels on this Kindle, the device has accumulated a long list, hundreds of words that I should have been studying all along. At this point it's just too many. Anyway, who needs to study when with the touch of a finger you can translate a word?

Unless, you know, you want to *remember* those words.

When I was eighteen I was in a car wreck and broke both legs. I had to spend four months not walking, mostly confined to a hospital bed. It was like house arrest. This was pre-Kindle, pre-tablet, pre-computer, pre-cable TV, pre-VCR; pre-pre. To kill time I read a lot of books. While I read, I decided to work on my vocabulary. I fancied myself becoming bookish. Of necessity, my approach was old school. Set the book down, pick up a dictionary, look up the word and its definition; go back to the book and resume reading. It was a long interruption.

After doing this for a while I found myself looking up some of the same words a second, third, even fourth time. These repeated visits to the dictionary, the repetitive motion of setting my book down and looking up the word and then setting the dictionary down and going back to my book, in short, the work and the interruption and, above all, the forgetting, got on my nerves. I started writing down words and definitions, keeping a list and *looking* at the list. I looked at it every day. In short order I could feel my vocab burgeoning.

Now it's happening all over. I look up some of the same words in Italian again and again. Why can't I remember? *Sconvolgere*. I've looked that word up (easily, instantaneously, with the flick of a finger) fifteen to twenty times. To devastate. To move deeply. Just now, writing this essay, I actually looked up *sconvolgere* again.

I've wiped Kindle's hard drive so I can start a new vocabulary list. I don't want hundreds of words. I only want a few words at a time. It's like my socks.

Her name is Corinne. Through the real estate office Antonio—he calls himself Mauro—arranges to meet his daughter at an apartment he pretends he wants to buy. He finds wily ways of eliciting personal information. He wants to know but cannot directly ask: What did her mother tell her? Does she know who her father was? Antonio/Mauro asks himself, Should I tell her?

His heart is in the right place, but things get a little creepy. He watches her come and go at her apartment. He follows her to breakfast and lunch and arranges surprise visits. They have dinner. They go to bars and clubs. Before each meeting he tells himself: this is it. Tonight I'll tell her. *I am your father.* Then he doesn't.

"Never memorize something you can look up." I'm glad Einstein said that. It lets me off the hook. Except Einstein was talking about stuff you'll need to know only once in a while. It takes Jupiter 4,333 days to orbit the sun. The square root of 13 is 3.6055512755. The melting point of Xenon is −169.2°F (−111.8°C). A lot of those Italian words I might not need again for a long time, maybe never. The word for snout, for example, I could just look up when I needed it.

But there's all kinds of stuff, basic factual stuff, we need to know or we want to know. And the more the better. The speed of light would be important to Einstein. The Italian verb *sconvolgere* has become important to me (along with a number of other words).

Conventional wisdom these days is that devices make us lazy and diminish us. A few years back Nicholas Carr made a number of trenchant observations on that subject in the *Atlantic Monthly* (see "Is Google Making Us Stupid?"). Kids especially, the argument goes, remember less because they don't have to remember. They have a short attention span, no mental muscles, no capacity to concentrate and remember. The opposing view is that devices free us to remember and think about other things. We free up cerebral disk space. So what if I no longer remember twenty-five phone numbers. My phone remembers them. So what if I ask Google for the population of Burundi and then forget it. I'm busy thinking about other things. (Just don't ask me what those other things are right now.)

Antonio/Mauro and Corinne go together to the Atlantic shore for the weekend (separate rooms). The more he sees her, the more he likes her, *loves* her. The better he gets to know his daughter, the more he wants to compensate for his absence from her life up to that time. But: If he tells her the truth, she might hate him.

In the corner of my device, Kindle indicates I've read 75 percent of the story. For a long time I missed seeing page numbers. I missed seeing the cover of the book. Half the time I can't tell you the title of the book I'm reading. I open my Kindle cover and there I am, on 45 percent. I'm not sure who the author is. (But I can find out if I need to know.)

"Our hominid ancestors may have cooked food . . . which made it softer." So says Jordi Marcé-Nogué, an expert on jaw evolution in primates at the University of Hamburg, adding, "That contributed to changes in the shape of the skull and mandible, which made way for a more complex brain." It was a big step in human evolution, an inflection point. More complex brain meant, eventually, more complex language. Forest and figs. And, thousands of years later, filigree and falafel.

We may be at another inflection point today, with the device-ification of human thought. What will the long-term impact of digital technology be? Maybe Google is making us stupid. Or maybe, as Andy Clark, at University of Edinburgh, and David Chalmers, at the Australian National University, argue, computer and tablet and smartphone and Google are all part of "extended mind." Mind, as they characterize it, is "a system made up of the brain plus parts of its environment." Your diary is extended mind. It helps you remember stuff. Your spouse, they argue, is extended mind. She helps you remember stuff. And now your smartphone and computer are extended mind. Maybe we shouldn't be alarmed.

I'm at 90 percent, still waiting for Antonio/Mauro to say the words "I am your father." "Sono tuo padre." "Je suis ton père." Contrary to what the title says, *Per nessun motivo*, he has his reasons for delay, among them, getting me to hang on until the end of the story.

The end of the story—I'm won't spoil it for you—is outrageous.

When I scan my new word list on my factory-reset Kindle, I'm surprised to see how many words I looked up in an hour or two of reading. A dozen or more. Which words do I really need? *Ardesia* (slate, as in slate roof). *Brusio* (hum, babble). *Prua* (prow or bow of a boat). *Pedinare* (to shadow, dog, tail). *Sbronzo* (plastered, sloshed). *Proboscide* (snout). Do I need to know these words?

How do we know what we need to know?

Honestly, I can probably get along without some of them. Though with a little study (flash card me, Kindle) I can acquire them. A little study. A little daily effort. There's an old-fashioned concept for you. Do the work. Love the device; do the work. Look at the word list every time I go to Kindle. Concentrate on the higher frequency look-ups (sconvolgere), extending my mind to Kindle. With time and effort, my Italian vocabulary could *germogliare* (burgeon), though that's a word, like *proboscide*, I may never need. To know them for now is good enough.

15 / Take the Money

In Italy, ATM. Always.

They call it Bancomat over here. It's fast. There's no talking involved. You take the money and run. Yesterday I had to go to the bank in San Marino. Into the bank. It's difficult to get in there. And even harder to get out.

Just push the button, you think. No, it's not that easy.

You're standing outside the Cassa di Risparmio, in front of a security system that's been in place, not just in San Marino but all over Italy, since local terrorism in the 1970s. Next to the entrance is a panel of secure lockers where you're supposed to stow any bags you're carrying. The green push button activates a reinforced steel door, which opens and admits you into a secure cylinder. You step in. The door slides shut behind you.

You wait, in what feels and looks like a giant pneumatic tube, wondering if, with a rush of air, you'll be transported into or ejected from the bank.

A mechanical lady says, in Italian, "Hold on just a second."

You wait.

She says, "Please go back outside and put your bag in the locker."

But, you think. But I need the stuff in my bag for this transaction to take place. Can you make an exception?

You wait. The door behind you does not open. Is she scanning you? Reconsidering? Inside, through the bullet-proof glass, you see three tellers and half a dozen clients waiting. Then, click, the inside door slides open. You enter, bag and all.

There's an air of importance about tellers in Italian banks. As if their real job is counting huge piles of money, banknotes in large denominations, in the inner sanctum of the bank. That and adjusting the levers of economic power with great delicacy and precision. But for the moment you're here, and they have to take care of you. When they're ready.

One of my first encounters with this attitude was in Florence, years ago. Back in the traveler's check era. Before the euro. I slowly passed through security, waited a long time in line, and presented myself to a teller. He had tired eyes and carefully combed salt and pepper hair. He was smoking a cigarette.

I told him I would like to cash traveler's checks, please.

He took a long puff on his cigarette and turned a blank look in my direction, a look relieved only slightly by raised eyebrows that said, How much?

Forty dollars.

He shrank from me. Forty dollars. And I felt ridiculous. Why not fifty? Why not sixty? His look suggested that another bit of non-renewable life force had been withdrawn from his person.

I signed my checks, he presented me with a form, tapping the space where I would provide my signature, then laid bills and a few coins on the counter, £68,680.

Wow, thanks. In the pile of cash, ten thousand lire notes. I, for one, felt increased by the transaction.

Today in San Marino the atmosphere is about the same. Among patrons there is an atmosphere of bored anxiety, such as you might find in a hospital ER waiting room. What talk there is occurs in hushed tones. For those who can't stand for long, the bank has provided a couple padded benches. There's no real line. We are more like an organized clump. Italians hate lines. Outside, in the non-bank world, they will cut a line in the blink of an eye. I've seen nuns do it. Not in a bank. Cut the line and you could be thrust into the pneumatic tube and expelled.

Each of the three tellers is busy with a patron, taking time out to talk on the phone for long intervals, striding away from their post to fetch forms.

When my turn comes, in only ten minutes, I've been mentally rehearsing what I will say in Italian. I've left my SMAC card home, in the United States. It's a card that gets me reward points for every purchase I make in San Marino, translating into euros I can spend in San Marino. I figure I have a couple hundred SMAC points. We're going to buy an electric tooth brush! We'll accumulate more SMAC this month. But I need a replacement card.

The teller is male, fashionably bald, fashionably scruffy. He opens my passport, clacks at the computer keyboard, finds my account. I make my little speech.

There are days when my Italian comes out smoothly. I can say what I want without effort. Other days it's halting and disjointed. Getting out of bed in the morning, I'm never quite sure which day it is. Last night in the bakery, I struggled to buy bread. It's part jet lag, part incapacity, part old age. Across my forehead, "foreigner" might as well be stamped. In the cell phone store they say things I don't understand. It's bad in banks, too.

So far, today is pretty good. I hand him the SMAC form and envelope that came with the card four years ago, which I have saved, miraculously, and kept in our apartment. He listens to my rehearsed speech, then nods in recognition. He works in silence for a moment, then says, "Do you have your TIN?" Sounds like *teen*.

"My what?"

"Your TIN." He tells me what that is, in Italian. I have no idea what he says, what he wants, what I need to get my SMAC and get the hell out of here.

In halting English he says: "Sochal Say-cur-ee-tee."

"Yes!" I say. "Yes, I do have that." I know my Social Security number. And I know my numbers in Italian. I begin saying my Social Security number in Italian. Tre otto due . . .

"No," he says. "I need the card. I have to make a copy."

Who carries that thing around? I know I had one when I was ten years old. "TIN," I say. Now I get it. Tax identification number.

"I have to keep track," he says, looking at his computer screen. "There is a campo to fill in. In San Marino there is a TIN. In Italy there is a TIN. In Europe countries you have a TIN." He pauses, gives me a look. What about my TIN? Campo. Of course: field, computer, international finance. Welcome to the New World Order.

I tell him I don't carry a Social Security card. In the United States we just say the number.

"Is this it?" he says, turning his computer screen toward me. It's my Medicare card they photographed a few years ago. So I'm already in the system. I'm a player. "Is okay?"

Yes, okay.

He says a replacement card costs ten euros.

I sign a few forms, he hands me my new card. Out of curiosity I ask: Can he tell me how many points I have on SMAC? He takes the form I'm holding, points at the bottom. 860 euros. What? I think. 860 euros? Holy cow, that's lot. I feel like Tom Hanks in *Big*, when he gets his first grown-up paycheck.

So that's it. I exit the bank through a different pneumatic tube. Push the button, step inside, one door closes, another one opens. I come away humbled and rattled, satisfied and surprised. It feels like progress. Usually I am just humbled and rattled.

When I was a kid, in my small-town bank, I walked up to a teller window and did business with Bob Hartley or Ruth Bennett. I had a paper route. Saturdays I deposited my weekly earnings— four dollars, five dollars, six dollars—in Freeland State Bank. We chatted, there were forms, signatures, initials. The friendly transaction, such as it was, proceeded. Will I ever come to feel that way in this small town in San Marino, in the Cassa di Risparmio in Serravalle? Somehow I doubt it.

I walk home thinking about SMAC, about the 860 euros. Way more than I thought. Then it occurs to me: that was not our SMAC balance, it was our bank balance, in an account we use to pay the lights, water, and gas bills when we're not here. International finance. I'm a player, all right. I'm in for 860 euros. Plus SMAC.

A pittance.

Like my forty dollars in traveler's checks.

But the teller, I didn't catch his name, was friendly and patient.
For now I'll call him Bob. And I'll be sure to look for him next time.

But not soon, I hope.

16 / Listen to Teresa

My wife is talking about Druids.

We're in a kitchen store in Rimini, a place where we buy stuff for our apartment—pans, glasses, cutting board, a new espresso pot. The lady there also keeps us supplied in stainless steel coasters, an accessory my wife delights in buying. (I do not. With the least bit of condensation from a cold drink, they stick to the bottom of a glass, then detach and cymbal crash on the tabletop when you take a drink.) Our cupboard back in the United States is full of them. Today the store is having a sale on nonstick pans, ten euro. We're tempted.

"Oh yes," my wife says. "The origins of Halloween actually can be traced back to the Druids."

The lady at the counter shakes her head. She has never heard of the Druids, which occasions a short disquisition on Celtic religion, one of my wife's many favorite subjects. She knows her stuff.

While she talks, I shop.

"Do you have any wine bottle stoppers?" I ask.

"Here," the lady says, pointing to a bin in front of the cash register. "On sale for three euro. One that draws air from the bottle, preserving the wine. The other, a simple stopper."

"On the occasion of the Celtic new year," my wife is saying, "which was the first of November, the dead returned and walked the earth."

I tell the lady I would like two simple ones.

"People dressed up in scary costumes and played tricks."

"We tried Halloween in Italy a few years ago," the lady says.

"I see pumpkins," I say. Albeit little ones, compared to the giants we grow in the United States.

"First year it was all Halloween, everywhere you looked. Next year a little less Halloween. Next year hardly anything. I guess it's just not part of our religion."

"But you have the day of the dead," my wife says. "The first of November."

Do they ever. The dead are huge in Italy.

So important that the day of the dead has become attenuated, fortunately, becoming the month of the dead. I say fortunately because the local bakeries turn out *fave dei morti*, beans of the dead, which are small almond-flavored cookies laced with anise; and *piada dei morti*, cakes of the dead, a confection with a flour and wine must base, mixed with dried fruit, pine nuts, walnuts, and cooked almonds, all baked and then slathered with honey. The bakeries do a big business around November 1, as do the cemeteries.

Every time we come to Italy and San Marino, regardless of the time of year, my wife and I walk up to the cemetery and visit our dead. This year I do double duty. After our visit, I am pressed into service by my wife's old aunt, who lives up the street from us. Her Ukrainian *badante* (live-in helper) and I will drive up to the *mercato* in Borgo Maggiore to buy flowers for all the family tombs, then dust and wash the stones and arrange the flowers.

The aunt, ninety-three years old, is the last of her generation. Every visit with her is like an audience with royalty. She sits in a stuffed leather chair in her *salotto*, dressed in a wool skirt, shoes and stockings, blouse and wool sweater, a wool shawl draped over her shoulders. She refers to herself in the third person, speaks with precision about the lady up the street cuckolded by her husband, about the opprobrious (her word) government officials that have ruined the republic and should be locked up, about her nephew Natalino, who weighed six kilos when he was born ("so big people from all over the hospital came to look at him"). Today Lena and I get exact instructions on what flowers to buy, which flowers go in front of which tomb, and how much cleaning solution to apply to gravestones.

"I think fifty euro should be enough," Lena says, thumbing bills from an envelope.

"No," the aunt says, "listen to Teresa. You will need at least seventy euro."

"I don't know," Lena says.

"No!" the aunt protests again. "Listen to Teresa."

Almost every visit, I ask her about a recipe: how she cooks a rabbit, her tuna sauce, the rice salad my wife loves. Before Lena and I go, Teresa repeats a recipe for turkey breast cooked in milk.

"Three or four slices of turkey breast," she says, "like this." She holds up her hand to demonstrate the size. "Slice them lengthwise into strips, like this." She holds up two fingers together to indicate the size. "Season them with a little oil, salt and pepper and marjoram. Let them rest overnight in the refrigerator. If you like garlic, sauté a small clove in oil, then gently cook the turkey slices, each side until the slices are white. Next you add the milk."

"How much?" I ask.

"Just enough," she says. She holds up two crooked fingers. "Two times. You add milk two times. Add enough milk to cover the slices in the pan. Raise the flame and cook the milk down. When it starts to get sticky, add the same amount of milk again, with just a little water to keep the milk from getting gooey. Cook the milk down again."

"Covered or uncovered?"

"Uncovered," she says. "Teresa cooks everything uncovered."

Cooking time, she says, is about thirty minutes. I'll try the recipe in my new nonstick pan.

I ask if she gets turkey at the butcher up the street.

She nods. "Tell him Teresa sent you."

Lena and I drive up to the local cemetery, through a stretch of what was once a train tunnel where locals took shelter from Allied bombing during the war. On the way we talk in Italian, with our odd accents. She's in her fifties, a widow ten years now, with all her family back in the Ukraine. She says she has no income, no pension, so she works here in San Marino, where there is an aging population and brisk business for *badante*.

"It's a war in my country," she says. "Very bad."

We buy potted yellow and white chrysanthemums, cut flowers, and a small cyclamen to take home to Teresa. The cemetery is crowded. People walk purposefully to their relatives' grave sites, draw water from the faucet into small buckets, and wipe down the stones, most of which are in above-ground crypts, with photographs of the deceased above the names and dates. Using a paintbrush designated for the job, I dust the family tombs; Lena then washes them. All around are names I have come to recognize, friends and relatives of my wife's family. Galassi, Berti, Franciosi, Casadei, Guidi, Marcucci, Mularoni.

Below my wife's grandparents are two tombs that haven't been visited in a while. Lena washes the one on the right, I take the one on the left.

"Our little act of mercy today," she says.

We walk in silence back to the car, surrounded by these deliberate acts of memory, a ritual so central to Italian life.

"Seventy euro," she said. "Teresa was right." Adding, "Remember the turkey. It's very good."

I will. There is so much to remember.

17 / Anyone Who Had a Heart

So my wife has it in for Burt Bacharach. We're driving down to Rimini this morning, where we'll visit the Grand Hotel, have some lunch, then go to the newly restored Fulgor movie theater to buy tickets to see the newly restored version of Fellini's *Amarcord*. And we're going to stock up on Jesuses at the Catholic accessory shop today.

At the moment we're sitting at one of the many stoplights between San Marino and Rimini. I tell her I have a song stuck in my head, "We've Only Just Begun."

"Good God," she says. "Why?"

"I thought of the song on our wedding anniversary," I say. That was yesterday.

"What bull," she says.

It is, in fact, a total load of bull. The song came to mind when I was in the bathroom a few days ago, thinking hopefully about one of the challenges of international travel—the time change, the change in diet and schedule, eating lunch when you usually eat breakfast, eating dinner when you usually eat lunch, eating a lot, I mean *a lot* more than usual. It's a thorough-going alteration of your input-output regimen. And that morning, well, signs were finally pointing in the right direction in the output department. Sitting there, feeling optimistic, I sang, "We've only just begun."

"Did Burt Bacharach write that?" she says now.

"Parts of the song sound like him," I say. "There's a really nice chord change at the bridge. Here—" I sing it: "Sharing horizons that are new to us. Watching the signs . . ."

"That's Burtish," I tell her. Pleased with my coinage.

Thinking of the song, and then hearing it, really pisses her off. She begins to excoriate Burt Bacharach. Burt Bacharach! My wife can be a monster. When I tell her that he wrote music, not lyrics, she says she doesn't care. The song is sappy, it's senti-mental, it's Burt Bacharach crap.

We ride along, alone in our thoughts. I start to hum, then stop, deciding to keep the Carpenters, and Burt, if it's Burt, to myself.

"My ears have been ringing a lot," I say. "Do you think there's a correlation between air travel and tinnitus?"

"I need to buy at least three Jesuses this year," she says.

A few minutes later I park our rental car, a car named Karl (no kidding), down by the beach, half a block from the hotel. It's just Karl and a Mercedes, side by side. When I check the Mercedes dashboard, I can see the driver didn't pay to park. I don't either. This is living dangerously.

We're here to look at rooms for a trip I'm planning a year from now. The hotel is legendary. It's palatial. It's art nouveau. High ceilings, arches, columns. A man wearing white gloves meets us at the door. I tell him we have an appointment, whereupon he shows us to the coffee bar. While we wait there he brings us first Claudio, then Violetta (he says "Wioletta"), then Eleonora.

Claudio says, "You've been coming to Rimini forty years and you've never been in the Grand Hotel?"

That's right. We've never really needed a hotel, I say. But if we did, it would be this one.

Wioletta shows us half a dozen rooms. At the Grand Hotel, there are no regular rooms. The bargain room is called an exec-utive room. Then come deluxe suites, very deluxe suites, and the extremely deluxe suite, named for Fellini, which has two baths, two bedrooms, and a spacious sitting room. On the wall outside the room is a photo portrait of the great director, wear-ing a clown nose.

Back at the front desk I tell Eleonora we'll need seven rooms, an assortment: a few executives, mostly deluxes.

And what sort of trip is this? she wonders.

Sights, I say. Roman ruins, hill towns, food and wine, probably some shopping. "I try to get people off the beaten path," I tell her.

She promises to hold rooms for our dates. On the way out, white gloves gets to the door before us, holds it open. He remembers my name.

Next up, my wife goes Jesus shopping.

"We've only just begun" is still playing in my mind.

At the next parking lot, over by the Tiberius bridge, we're approached by a couple African men, as usual. Lots of begging in Italy, lots of need, gradations of desperation we can't even begin to imagine. There's gypsies, out-of-work types; also, judging by their clothes, a few prefer-not-to-work types, most of whom appeal to you from a kneeling position, avoiding eye contact. Very common, especially in parking lots, are the Africans. It's good to have coins in your pocket.

The Africans work on their feet. Some of them show you where there are parking spots, then guide you into your spot. They want to be paid for that. Others just stand near the pay meter and ask for money. They call me "capo," which my wife hates. "Do you have a coin, boss?" they say. I have no idea how they live—what they eat, where they sleep, where the Africans at the stoplights get those packets of Kleenex they want to sell you. At the stoplights I hold up a hand and shake my head no. In the parking lot they're right there in front of you. Young and middle-aged men. You never see women.

"Sell what you possess, and give alms." Thus sayeth the scripture (Luke 12:31).

Reserve hotel rooms, and give alms. I do. What else are coins are for?

Crossing the bridge, I say to my wife, "Okay if I don't go in the Catholic shop?"

It's actually called Semprini Arredi Sacri, sacred articles, right around the corner from Rimini's cathedral. They have something for everyone. Would you like a life size statue of Padre Pio? A crucifix magnet? An Ave Maria key chain? A guardian angel nightlight? Some grappa from the local monastery? There's also a full array of priest- and nun-wear and liturgical hardware, though I think you need a license to buy stuff like that.

And nativity stuff. That's my wife's bag.

"What about Francesco?" she says. He's her go-to guy at Semprini, about forty, thin, a few days' growth of beard, always smelling of cigarette smoke. I like him. But I can only take so much of the store's oppressive iconography. It's how I picture purgatory.

I tell her I'll go have a glass of wine at I Putti and wait for her there.

I Putti—meaning the angels—is our new wine bar. At 11:45 I have a glass of Sangiovese. After my second sip, Marco sets down a small pizza and a smaller prosciutto sandwich. I know man does not live by bread alone, but this bread and this wine get awfully close to holiness.

She'll be a while, I tell Marco when he asks about my wife. The Jesuses are for some nieces and nephews back home, the nativity sets my wife equips them with. The problem is, they keep losing their Jesus.

While it's just me I take out my phone and google Burt. How about that? Burt Bacharach, I find, is still alive and kicking at ninety-one. Married four times. His memoir is titled *Anyone Who Had a Heart*. That's also a song. He wrote that, too? I love that song. I dig a little further. "Say a Little Prayer," of course. Come to find out, he did not write "We've Only Just Begun." On the sound system I Putti are playing American rock and roll. They've probably never heard of Burt Bacharach or the Carpentieri.

The door clicks open and my wife comes in. "Hey," she says, looking crestfallen.

"Jesuses?"

She shakes her head. "They were busted."

"How?"

"Just ugly. Francesco says he'll be getting more in."

"Don't want no ugly Jesus," I say.

She picks up a tiny bite of pizza, pops it in her mouth, and shakes her head. Yes, it's a low-level religious experience. She points at my glass. Yes, sure, I say, try the wine. This is communion. We sit, satisfied, sanctified. I wait a few minutes. Then, I have to tell her. I can't help myself.

"It's not Burt Bacharach who wrote that song," I say. "It's a guy named Paul Williams. Remember him? A little guy with glasses?"

"I don't care," she says. "I still hate that song."

"How about 'Anyone Who Had a Heart?' That's a good song."

"I don't know it."

"Burt Bacharach at his best." I'm on a roll. I sing her the first few notes of "Do You Know the Way to San Jose." The *wuh-wuh-wuh-wuh-wuh, wuh-wuh-wuh-wuh-wuh, wuh, wuh*. It's cheerful, but I know I'm pushing it now.

"Dreadful."

"Good tune. That's Burt's work."

The day is still young. We'll have seafood risotto at Trattoria Marianna, then go to the theater for our tickets. We get the last two seats, up in the balcony. Good for some anniversary making out up there, I tell her.

The next morning, lodged in my brain, will be the theme song from *Amarcord*, sweet and kind of seasick. Every bit as sticky as that other song.

18 / Drop It

I find a flyer on my mailbox for La Poo Perfect. In quotation marks, their tagline: "Don't stoop. We'll scoop." They have daily, weekly, monthly plans. The woman who answers the phone is named Sam. "Kinda dog?" she says. Her voice is deep, cigarette husky. I tell her I don't have a dog, and no, I'm not calling for a friend or neighbor. Long pause, Sam breathing.

"I wanted to ask," I say, "do you deliver?"

Sam lets go a gooey laugh. She has a sense of humor—she answers the phone "La Poo." But I'm not joking. For weeks I've been flinging turds into the street. Every time I cut the grass I find them. I put a couple sticks together and chopstick the poo onto the road. The other day I had to get a shovel. We're talking kielbasas. Then I find La Poo's flyer. It got me thinking.

"Deliver?" Sam says. "Lemme get Eddie."

Eddie gets on the phone. "You want what?"

"Poo," I tell him. "I want poo. Delivered." I hear Sam's phlegmy laugh in the background.

"We don't usually deliver," Eddie says. "We take it off people's hands." And their feet. Of course, I say, you get rid of the stuff.

"Mind if I ask why you want it?"

I tell him, yes, I do mind. Why is it important?

"From a business perspective," he says, "I should know what you're doing with our product."

"When you toss it in the street like that," my wife says one night, "the wrong people might step in it. Have you thought about that? What about Madelen?"

She's right. I would hate for Madelen's adorable foot to be soiled, Madelen with such extraordinary grace and equipoise, she should be in paintings. No, that wouldn't do. But there's neighbors and then there's neighbors. I ask my wife what I should do with it then.

"Deal with it."

I tell her that's glib and dismissive.

"When you were a kid," she says, "you had a dog. Where did it go?"

I'm not sure. What I think is: Mrs. Compton's yard. What I say is: Down by the river. "I grew up in a small town," I say. "We had wilderness."

She says I'm making a big deal over nothing.

"Obviously," I tell her, "you have not danced the dog poo pas de deux."

"That's two dancers," she says, smartassy.

"Me and the lawnmower," I smartass back.

Eddie puts me on hold, presumably so he and Sam can discuss the niceties of their product. The term makes it sound like a commodity that's packaged and stored. I picture warehouses full of cooling devices to keep the product stable. Eddie clicks back on the line. "How much you need?"

What's the unit of measurement? "Five gallons?" I say.

"Gallons," he says.

"Yeah, you know, like ice cream?"

I wonder if they feel a twinge of regret when they drive past my house. Thinking: that's where Bruno dumped. I hope he didn't step in it. Meaning me. Or do they lie awake at night, examining their wrongdoing, their flouting of common courtesy. I don't think they do. Probably they think, Tonight we will visit the other street. So many streets, so many guilt-free deposits. No twinge of regret. This emboldens me.

I shop Amazon.com, Cheaperthandirt.com, and find something called EyeClops Night Vision Infrared Stealth Goggles. I have all the evidence I need. I can't cut my grass without stepping in it. I would like to see the perp in action. I have suspicions. I need certainty. Night goggles are expensive.

How do you know it happens at night? my wife asks. We're lying in bed. I'm staring at the front window. Right now the nightwalkers are out there. She sets down her book. "Maybe they do it early in the morning," she says.

"Vandals," I say, "do not get up early."

"Night goggles?" she says. "You're turning into a nutcase vigilante."

I can't walk in my yard barefoot. It's time to draw a line in the grass.

A neighbor has a lawn sign, Ryan for probate judge, "Protecting our families." What does that mean? "Guarding our lawns" I might vote for. It's specific.

One night my wife and I come home late. The woman who put the sign out is standing by our mailbox. She's walking a black dog the size of pony. If I roll down the window and say, "You're bagging it, right?" I'm a bad neighbor. I don't. I'm pretty sure she doesn't.

Tonight I'm standing by the front door. It's almost dark. I look down toward the street. What's this but a golden retriever assuming the position. This is it. I elbow the door open, step off the porch. A girl holding the leash watches me come. The closer I get, the clearer it becomes that she doesn't get it. She's smiling. The dog finishes, does his little cleanup scratch, and assumes a regal sit next to the girl.

"Well?" I say.

"Hello," she says, very breezy. "Watch out or the mosquitoes will bite." She sounds foreign.

"What are you doing?" I say.

"Tonight I walk the dog."

"I can see that," I say. "But this?" I point.

"Oh, that," she plugs her nose and laughs, then holds out her hand. "Justine," she says. "I'm from France." She says *Fronce*. I shake her hand.

"Don't people in Fronce clean up a mess like this?"

"In the city, yes," she says, then adds with a guilty laugh, "but only sometimes."

"Here we always do," I say. It's a lie, but I'd like to set a high standard. "Always," I say again, almost ready to give her *toujours*. She shakes her head no.

"Here is the country, no?"

No, I say. We have lots of trees and grass, but no, this is not the country. The dog nudges my leg, then sniffs my crotch. I know this dog. It's the Buckleys'. And this Justine must be an au pair.

"We pick up," I say again.

Justine tenses. She looks at me, eyes narrowing. Then: "I see."

She's got the hauteur, and I've got the poo. It's sort of a standoff. I'm not enjoying it. It's not what I imagined. I'm thinking it will pass, and then Justine does something terrible. She squares her shoulders, draws in her lower lip, whispers, "Okay." She reaches behind her, I see a flash of white as she produces a tissue. When she whips it open, I see it's a handkerchief.

A little French handkerchief, clean and white, with a colored border.

"It's all right," I say.

But it's too late. Justine bends down, reaches out, and picks up the dropping with her hankie. She straightens, sniffs, and I realize she's crying. The thought of that dreadful thing in her hand, warm as a croissant, makes me so sick that I now want to cry, or throw up, or both. She clicks her tongue at the dog. They go.

I'm cutting the grass the next morning when I see a vehicle crawl down the street. Twice it noses to a stop in front of a house, then starts up. The driver's looking for someone. I watch as it pulls in my driveway. It's a rusty old Mazda, half van, half car, kind of a dusty hippo gray. I shut my mower down as the driver's door screeches open. A little guy in army fatigues gets out. He's got a mess of blue tattoos up and down his arms.

"Help you?" I say.

He nods and smiles, smoothing his long black mustache with a forefinger. He could be thirty or fifty. He walks across the lawn in army boots, holds out his hand to shake. "Eddie," he says. "Eddie Swit from Poo Perfect?" I shake his hand. "Got your order," he says.

My order.

You know, I want to say, that idea I had, my heart is no longer in it. But he's already swung around, walking back to his car.

He opens the Mazda hatch, reaches in, and lifts out a white bucket. There's a lid on the bucket. A yellow invoice is taped to the side of it. I'd like him to put it right back, shut the hatch, and forget about the whole thing. Eddie crosses his tattooed arms and smiles.

"Look, Eddie," I say.

"Five gallons," he says, "is what you ordered." He nudges the pail with his boot. "Just like ice cream." It occurs to me we didn't talk price.

When I tell him I don't want it, he pulls on his mustache again and says, "You know what I had to do to get this? Do you have any idea?" I tell him yes, I know what he had to do. "No, you don't," he says. "You just bag it and toss it. This was collection and consolidation." He nudges the bucket again with his boot. "Consolidation." A neighbor goes walking by. I'm glad Eddie has an unmarked truck.

"I expect to be paid," he says.

I have a pretty good idea what will happen if I don't pay. I'll come out one morning and find a pile on my lawn, a big pile, like five gallons. And maybe not just once. Maybe repeatedly. Until he feels I've learned a lesson. He seems like that kind of guy who would teach someone a lesson.

I point at the bucket. "Is it sealed?"

"Tight," he says.

"How about I pay and you just take it back."

Eddie shakes his head no. I pay for the bucket of product. Eddie can't make change, so he ends up with a tip. I carry the bucket into the garage, put it in a corner, and watch Eddie drive away.

That night I lie awake, picturing unimpeded nightwalkers stopping by out front, remembering the terrible Justine episode. Mostly I think about the bucket down in the garage, the contents hermetically sealed, deliquescing. It's pure evil.

19 / Teeth First

"Tuesday is tooth day," my wife has been saying.

For a year now, I've been waiting on a new tooth. A front tooth, a lower incisor, what I call a biter. In college I tended to use my teeth as pliers. Sewing a button on a pair of jeans one day, I clamped onto a needle with my teeth to pull it through a tough knob of denim. The needle was stuck. When I bit down and pulled, my tooth made a little crunch sound. Last year it finally crumbled in my mouth and became a hole in my smile. I wore a partial thingy, a temporary tooth, for a while. Its plastic chafed my tongue, so I kept the partial in my pocket, taking it out in case I needed my dignity, which, fortunately, is rare these days.

Today I get my new tooth, an implant. At last, it's Tuesday.

"So you're going back to her," she says. She's eating an egg, I'm spooning down a bowl of cereal. It's August, already hot at 7:00 a.m. Hot makes my wife cross.

"Yes, and that kid's coming today," I say.

"The great Dr. Franz," she says. My dentist also makes my wife cross. For a few years now, we've been waging dentist wars. Dr. Franz, she says, is old school and cavalier and charges too much. Her dentist, I say, is new school and holistic and practices voodoo dentistry. I don't know exactly what I mean by that, but it makes my wife angry when I say it. I keep it in reserve.

"What kid?" She holds her dish out for me to take to the sink, points at her coffee cup. "Please?"

"For the car," I say. "The one who might buy the car."

She snaps the opinion section of the newspaper, then smooths it across the table with the back of her hand.

"Is he buying it or not?"

It's an old Dodge our son drove. When he went off to New York to make his name, I put a sign on it with my phone number. Yesterday I'm on my second cup of coffee at the Panera when my phone rings.

"I'm calling about your car." A no-nonsense female voice.

"The Dodge?" I say. "I'm asking fifteen hundred."

"I saw it in the parking lot," she says.

I swallow a drink of coffee. "Where was that?"

"Right outside," she says, "just now. Where are you sitting?"

"What?" I lean over and look down the length of the restaurant. There's a priest down there reading the newspaper, also a couple business guys with their laptops open. Standing next to muffins is a woman in a beige linen suit. She has brown hair, sunglasses pushed up on top of her head.

"Hi there." She waves at me.

Hi, I say back. Then: "I should tell you, it's a stick."

She's walking toward me now, tall, willowy, still holding her phone to her ear. "It's not for me," she says. "I wouldn't get caught dead driving a car like that."

Then she's looming above me. She's tall, tan, and fragrant. She snaps her phone shut and drops it in her purse. I gesture toward the space across from me. "Who's it for?"

She slides into the booth, sets down a brown leather bag and a big jingle of keys.

In case of dignity, insert tooth. Too late for that.

She says she's looking for a car for her son, who's sixteen and just got his license. When I tell her again it's a stick, she says, "He thinks he wants the standard transmission." For some reason, she puts long finger quotation marks around *standard*.

Thinks he wants, I say.

"He doesn't know how to drive one."

"*Standard*'s a misnomer these days." I take another drink of coffee. "Maybe his father can teach him to drive it."

"That's not going to happen," she says. She lays an index finger on the table, the shiny red nail pointed at me. "Here's the deal. You teach him to drive it, you sell your car."

"It's not that hard," I say.

"Good." She's standing up. Then looming over me again she says. "How many offers have you had?"

"A couple," I lie.

She nods.

"He can learn to drive a stick," I say. "It's not that hard."

"Then it shouldn't take you long to teach him," she says. "How's tomorrow morning? His name is Brett."

Next day midmorning a black sedan wheels in our driveway. I step out on the front porch to make sure it's them, then walk down to the drive. Her window buzzes down. She looks at me over her sunglasses, wonders how much time I suggest. The boy's sitting in the passenger seat looking over the dash at my car.

"Hour," I say. "Make it two, to be safe."

She checks her watch, then puts her car in reverse. "Honey?" she says to the boy. He says something I can't hear, to which she responds, "It's a learner." At that, his door opens.

He's tall and thin, with short sandy hair. His eyelids are reddish. The temperature's on its way to ninety and humid; he's dressed in royal blue sweats. He walks around the front of the car, turns toward me, and squints.

"Brett," I say.

"Yeah." He swings around, looks at the car, then turns back to me. "I don't like to back up," he says.

I back the car down the driveway while he stands in the yard watching, like it's a mobile operating room and he's about to perform his first surgery. At the bottom of the driveway, I get out and walk around to the passenger side. He's a tall kid. He has to move the driver's seat back and forth a few times while I explain pedals and the idea of contrary motion. Down on the gas, up with the clutch. But gentle. The legend on the stick shift faded a long time ago, so I draw the shifting pattern on the dash. I tell him it's a five-speed. We'll just use first, second, and third for a while.

"Does the radio work?"

I tell him it does. He's not going to be happy about the speakers, I think, and decide to let him discover that. "Four-disk CD player," I add, anticipating his next question.

He turns the key in the ignition, nothing happens.

"It won't start," I say, "without the clutch in."

He shoves in the clutch, starts the engine, and blinks his red eyes.

"Mirrors good?" I ask.

He revs a couple times, looks at me, and smiles. He points at my mouth. "You play hockey or something?"

On the third try we get forward motion without stalling the engine. He can't get to second and third gear without a big noisy rev, which startles him. Contrary motion, I tell him. Ease the gas when you shove in the clutch. A little breeze flows through the car as he accelerates in third gear. I take him into the subdivision where I taught my kids to drive stick. We stop and start. He stalls out again and again. His face gets red with frustration and shame. "What the hell's wrong with this thing?" he says. I tell him it's doing exactly what it's supposed to do. He'll get it eventually. It's a feeling. When he gets it, he'll like it. For a few minutes of relief, I take him out on the road, where we accelerate with the windows down.

He eyes the switches above the radio. "AC work?"

"Like new." We cruise along in silence. "Pretty good?" I say. He smiles just a little. I ask him why he wants a car with a stick.

"I want to burn rubber," he says. He cups his hand on the shifting knob. I don't have the heart to tell him, this car probably won't do what he has in mind. "I want to do something those assholes at school can't."

The two-lane road we're on winds past a school. I tell him we'll go right at the next traffic light. "Ease off on the gas, clutch in," I say.

We coast along, past some wetlands, up to the intersection. I'm hoping the traffic light cooperates.

"Up into third," I say. We execute a little downshift. When I tell him to ease the clutch out, he pops it, throwing both of us into the dash. "Keep going," I say. "Remember, everything gentle. Gradual."

He attends an all-boy prep, he says, starting junior year. He doesn't like math, history sucks, he hasn't found a sport. Without a sport, he says, you're basically nothing at this school. He gets picked on.

"That's hard," I say. He nods.

I've been past the school plenty of times. Kids with cars way nicer than mine. I'm not sure how this car solves his problem.

Next intersection we have to make a left, which means waiting for oncoming traffic to clear.

"Pull into the intersection and stop," I say. "Put it in first, holding down the clutch." The light is green. We stop and wait as one, two, three cars pass. "You can wait for yellow, or if there's time, ease the clutch and make your turn."

"Damn," he says.

The light's still green. Car coming at us. Not enough time to make the turn. "Not yet," I say.

"Damn shit," he says. "This guy's on my ass." Behind us, a black suv.

"He can wait," I say. The light goes amber.

"What do I do?"

"Wait."

Our engine starts to rev. "What do I do?"

"Wait!" I say. I'm not sure the car coming at us will stop. "Just wait!"

The suv's horn blasts behind us, Brett pops the clutch, and we lurch through the intersection in first gear, completing the turn. The car coming at us noses to a stop, horn blaring. Just past the intersection Brett drives onto the shoulder and stops. The suv thunders past us, giving us another dose of horn to make sure we understand.

Brett shuts off the engine. He grips the steering wheel and starts shaking his head.

"Breathe," I say. At the side of the road is a ditch. It's full of cat-tails. On top of one, a red-winged blackbird is perched, swaying in the breeze. "You never have to go," I say, "in a situation like that. Just wait until it's safe. Wait until you're ready."

"This car sucks," he says. He's squeezing the steering wheel like he's going to rip it off and throw it out the window.

"You're getting the hang of it," I say. "In a couple days, you'll be shifting like a pro."

"This car totally sucks," he says. "I can't drive a piece of crap like this to school. I'll get laughed out of the parking lot."

"You burned a little rubber back there."

"I wanted a Cobra," he says. "A red one. A convertible. My old man said first I gotta learn to drive a stick. He calls it 'quid pro quo.' Drive an old piece of shit, beat the crap out of it learning how to drive. Then I'll be ready for a nice car." He pushes the button to turn on the radio. When nothing happens, he pushes it again, four or five times. "'Like when?' I say. 'When will that be?'"

"You're learning," I say. "It won't take long."

"A Dodge," he says, shaking his head.

"Cobra's a nice car," I say.

"With a stick. And wide tires. And a v-8."

"That's a lot of power." I picture him pulling into that school parking lot, gunning the engine, squealing the tires, walking down the hall with the keys in his hand. But first he's going to ruin my car. His car. I know I shouldn't care. It's just metal.

We sit there a minute longer. The blackbird's gone. The air smells of hot ditch, kind of a good rotten smell. I take him back to the subdivision, where we do stops and starts on some hills. It does not go well. But then, it never does at first. He'll get it.

"Really?" his mother says.

"Really. I think he's going to be a natural."

Brett's leaning against the Dodge, seething.

"Did you hear that, honey?" his mother says. "A natural."

"Quid pro quo," he says.

"You said fifteen hundred?" She takes out her checkbook and starts to write a check. I stop her. I tell her I'm sure her check is good, but I'd feel better with a cashier's check. It's cleaner that way. It's the way business is done.

"Business," she says.

"Cashier's or certified check."

"This afternoon . . . ," she starts to say.

I tell her I'm tied up. We can meet tonight. It's the best I can do. Besides, I have to find the title.

Later that afternoon I'm in the dentist's chair, looking up Dr. Franz's nostrils, which she has a tendency to flair when she concentrates.

She says, "So you didn't like that partial I made for you."

"Not much."

She shakes her head, shows me my implant. "Good color match. I may have to grind it just a little, for a good fit." She pats my shoulder, something I like about her. "Won't hurt a bit."

"The truth is, I enjoyed going toothless," I say. "I have a friend who never wears socks. Weddings, funerals, whatever the occasion. No socks."

"Open." She slips the tooth in. Her nostrils flair. "A tooth is different," she says. "It's how you present yourself to the world. Once we get your mouth fixed up, I'm going to send you to Dr. Wheeler. He could help you with those eyelids." She slips the tooth back out.

I think about how we present ourselves to the world, teeth first. "My wife says I look like a beagle."

Dr. Franz is grinding.

"Droopy lids, sad eyes," I say.

"Does your wife like dogs?" she says. "Open." She's gluing the tooth in place. She turns it, taps it, presses down. I taste a bitter compound.

No, I would say if I could. She is not a dog person.

That night, to celebrate my tooth, we meet at Duffy's. I drive the Dodge; my wife drives her car. Brett's mother says she's heard of the place. She and Brett will meet us there to pick up the car.

I order a steak, something that will need a good biting.

"That's what bothers me about Dr. Franz," my wife is saying. "She's all about unnecessary procedures." She means my eyelids. I have no intention of getting my eyelids fixed. I've seen the aftermath, two black eyes. And for what? We eat and talk. I can't keep my tongue away from my new tooth. I definitely miss the gap. The new tooth fits, but it feels like it belongs in someone else's mouth.

"In a strong wind," I say, "I can feel my eyelids flutter."

She takes a drink of wine, sets her glass down. "Let me see that thing."

I smile at her. She leans across the table and looks. She asks how long it's supposed to last. Forever, I say. A lifetime guarantee. She says it looks good.

I'm half done with the steak, a good tough one, when my phone rings.

"You got the title, right?" The voice of Brett's mother.

I look around the restaurant. "Where are you?" I say.

There she comes, still wearing those sunglasses pushed up in her hair, a tall handsome woman who likes to own the room. She dumps her bag on the edge of the table, opens it, and pulls out an envelope.

"Brett?" I say.

"Brett's in the car," she says.

So he wouldn't come in, I think. He's still mad about getting the car he doesn't want.

"Had any more calls on that thing?" she says. I cut a bite of steak.

I don't like the way she says "thing." And I don't like the question.

"Is that a cashier's check?" I say, pointing at the envelope.

She pulls it out. "The problem is, Brett really doesn't like the car very much. And technically, it's just temporary." She hands me the check. "We're prepared to offer you twelve hundred."

I look at the check, smile at her, then hand it back.

"Do you want to think about it?"

I tell her no, I don't need to think about it.

"I checked the Blue Book."

"I don't think you did," I say. "But either way, I don't care. I'm no longer selling."

She lays the check on the table, opens the envelope, and takes out three crisp $100 bills. "You drive a hard bargain," she says. "I'll meet your price."

I shake my head. "The car's not for sale," I say. She looks at my wife, who shrugs and takes a drink of wine.

"We had a deal," Brett's mom says.

"Brett's a very angry boy," I say. "I wouldn't want to make things worse. As a gift to him, I've decided to keep the car."

She stands and stares at me. She wants the car. It feels good not selling it. She nods her head and slips the check and her bills back in the envelope. "Last chance."

"No charge for the driving lesson," I say.

She turns to go just as our waiter returns. He wonders if we'd like to hear the dessert specials. I'm thinking about that old piece of crap parked under a light in the lot, for sale signs still on the rear windows. I tell the waiter I'll have the cobbler.

Then I'll drive home with the windows down and the radio on, see if I can burn a little rubber.

20 / Back to Comanche

It's a big sucker. On the corner post of the back porch, there's this thing with wings, like a grasshopper, only four inches long. "Come look at this," I say to my wife. It's burger night, I've got the grill lit, but I'm thinking maybe we should just run. What if there are more?

"Creepy," she says.

"In a world man has destroyed," I say in movie-preview voice, "nature gets its revenge."

"You okay?"

I say yes. She knows I'm not.

"Maybe it'll turn into a butterfly," she says.

"In a cocoon the size of a football."

I grill the burgers. It's still there. We eat, then wash dishes. Still there. Later on, I go out with a flashlight. Still there, by itself. Big. My wife says, "I'll call Joann."

That afternoon I'm at Red Cross giving blood. Kandice does the Q and A. She comes in with a flourish of her synthetic gown. "Did you eat today?" she asks.

"Kandice with a K," I say. "You've been saying that your whole life."

She rolls her eyes. "How come you don't eat?"

"I just got back from Atlanta," I say. "I'm outta whack."

She wraps the blood pressure cuff around my arm, pumps me up. "Drive?"

"I saw a hundred dead deer on the road." I feel the blood bumping in my arm.

Kandice loosens the screw on the bulb and the cuff exhales. She says, "You're kinda high today. Alcohol?"

"A glass of wine. One a day."

She asks, I tell her about my coffee consumption. When I do the math, the number of espressos surprises me.

"You probably ought to cut back," she says.

"Wine or coffee?"

She smiles, for the first time. "I'd cut back on coffee first."

I get almost home, I notice this car behind me, up close and personal, a guy driving. I turn down my street, he turns too. Not a car I've seen in the neighborhood. I pull in my driveway, go halfway up the drive, and stop. This car, a white sports sedan, looks like a fang on wheels, it's parked at the bottom of the driveway. The guy has his window down, an arm dangling out of it. He might be looking for someone, I think. He might be lost.

I get out. "Help you?"

"You sonofabitch," he says, "you cut me off."

"What?" I say. "When? Where?" I think back a block, a mile, a day; nothing.

"Don't bullshit me." He raises that arm, levels his index finger at me. "You know you did," he says. "I oughta kick your ass."

"If I did," I say, "I'm really sorry."

"Sonofabitch." He says again that he should kick my ass, then steps on the gas and roars away. I stand there, baffled, and realize I'm shaking. I look up and down the street. No one outside. Just me and Badass.

Inside the house, I set a bag of groceries on the counter.

"Got any blood left?" my wife says.

"My blood pressure was high." I reach in the bag and pull out a bottle of wine. "I guess I need to cut down on coffee," I say.

"You gonna light the grill?"

"You'll never guess what just happened." I can still feel the adrenaline rush. I don't like it.

Our friend Joann the naturalist comes to the door in her pajamas. Bug books under her arm. There's a gleam in her eye that comes with the thrill of pursuit. Ask her, she'll tell you forty years ago she was a hippie. It's not difficult picturing her in jeans, beads, tie-dye, feathers in her hair. Now she works the school nature center, which means she talks to you like you're a sixth grader. The three of us walk through the house, out the back door onto the porch. She sets her books down on the table.

I hand her the flashlight. She puts on her glasses and looks.

"Oh my," she says. "Thank you so much for calling me."

I tell her it doesn't seem like a good idea, her driving around in her pajamas. My rolls her eyes. "You never know," I say.

"I was in bed," she says. "But I had to come. She'll be gone in the morning."

Both of us: "She?"

"She, yes. Notice the antennae. And notice her slightly distended abdomen." She tilts her head, draws close to the thing, a few inches away. "I'd say this is a polyphemus moth. She's sending out a powerful scent right now. Males of the species will detect it and come to her. They'll mate. In the morning she'll be gone."

This scent she sends out, I picture it, for some reason, as searchlights or laser beams boring into the night. "It's not going to eat the wood on the house," I say.

"It doesn't eat," she says. "The caterpillar eats. This moth procreates, then it dies."

"I think I know what happened," I say to my wife. We're lying in bed. She's reading a book about Cynthia Ann Parker, kidnapped by the Comanche in 1836. "I know where I cut him off."

"These guys were brutal," she says.

"On the corner of Franklin and Walnut Lake." I wait for a response. She's reading.

"Remember that TV commercial," she says finally, "the piles of garbage and the American Indian with a tear dropping from the corner of his eye?"

"Except I didn't cut him off."

"Pure revisionist history. A romanticized view of the American Indian," she says. "They raped, they murdered, they tortured people." She taps a page with her index finger and shakes her head. "Mutilation. Babies, slaughtered."

"There's that temporary right lane as you go through the light, north on Franklin?"

"The Comanche," she says, "were terrible."

"I was in that lane. He was in the main lane."

"Sometimes you drive too fast," she says. "You don't pay attention."

"He would proceed first. I drove past him on the right."

She reads for minute, then says, with genuine sadness, "So much for the noble savage."

"I must have startled him. Made him angry." I stare up at the ceiling, playing back the driveway encounter. He sat there, waiting for me to get out of my car. "He probably was waiting to see how big I was."

"What?"

"That guy this afternoon. What if I was big?"

"Let it go," she says.

"He sat there waiting. Because what if I was linebacker size? What if I was Del Durfee size?"

"Who's Del Durfee?"

"A guy I knew in high school." I realize I'm seething. "That guy'd've shut his trap and drove away."

We lie there a minute. I'm pretty sure I won't be able to sleep. And now I got blood pressure. She closes her book and shuts off her light. "They'd take women who looked like they could work, and a couple kids," she says. "Kill everyone else."

He was the sonofabitch.

Next morning on the way to work I stop at my coffee spot. I ask Taha what kind of tea they have.

"Tea?" He's already working on my double espresso.

"Something herbal."

He starts down the list, I'm listening for something I know, like Lipton. "Sweet cranberry fruit mélange, rooibos chai, Assam Mangalam . . ."

"Green tea," I say at last. "Plain."

Taha is a little Egyptian, with a voice so soft you have to lean over the counter to hear him. His manner is nothing if not cherubic. He also has a black belt in some variety of martial arts. He's told me what. To me it's all karate. Some Monday mornings his arms are red and bruised. Once he told me his jaw was dislocated. This morning I'm picturing Taha pulling a big guy out of a car, educating him, then throwing him in the ditch.

"Green tea," he whispers, handing me my drink.

"I'd like to see you fight sometime, Taha."

"I don't fight," he says. "I compete."

This thing of tea is big and hot. I hate it already. "But you could fight," I say.

He gives me a gentle smile. "I would do anything not to fight."

I stop in to see Sheldon at work, to tell him about the polyphemus moth. I know it will make his day. Sheldon is sixty, balding, an avid bridge player. Also a nature hog. He's walked the Appalachian Trail a few times. He plans to retire soon so he can devote himself to playing cards and hiking. There must be outward bound bridge tournaments somewhere. While we're talking, I begin to notice, for the third or fourth time, this little hallucination thing I've got going. Things are walking into and out of my peripheral vision, little bug-like things; there and gone. I suppose it's blood pressure.

I wonder out loud if I should see a doctor.

"Eat right," he says. "Nuts, celery. How's your omega-3s?"

How should I know?

"Get your fish oils going. Limit your industrial foods. There is a pestilence upon the land."

I tell him I appreciate both his advice and his biblical utterances. I've seen two doctors in the past ten years, a big one and a little one. The big one is your standard issue internal medicine man, an affable guy forty pounds overweight, with a ready prescription pad. The little one is the holistic guy. My wife calls him Speedy. He doesn't have an ounce of fat on him. He says to eat the way people ate in the 1700s. If you can't eat right, he can get the eighteenth century into you through the miracle of dietary supplements. Either way, you end up with artificial pills or natural pills. I don't like pills.

I ask Sheldon about his daughter, he shakes his head. "They rob her blind." She and her husband have orchards, cider, doughnuts, a specialty shop. "Last weekend," he says, "there were a couple men in the shop for over an hour." He looks out the window and shakes his head. "In security films, you can see guns in their pockets. People will do anything these days. They're so desperate."

They certainly seem crazy, I say.

"They'll kill and not even blink an eye."

I start to say it will be all right, but I'm not so sure. When I turn to go, I tell him I had green tea today.

"Polyphenols," he says. "Out with the free radicals."

"You know she wanted to go back," my wife says. We're lying in bed. She's reading about Cynthia Ann Parker and her daughter recaptured and repatriated to civilized life. I'm reading about hypertension. The story starts slow, then rises to a predictable and awful denouement. I'm also watching for phantom insects in my peripheral vision.

"Back to the Comanche?"

"Is that from the internet?" she says, pointing to my reading. "You should talk to Speedy."

"Maybe I will."

"Yes, the Comanche."

"Life was good," I say.

"It was the life she knew. She tried to escape from the white people. She ran away countless times. She cut her breasts with a knife, not to kill herself, but out of grief. Then her daughter died. Then she died."

I tell her I liked it better when she was reading about the Persians. "They made you laugh," I say.

"I can't believe you're giving up coffee."

"I'll be an herbal gerbil."

"I don't think you'll be able to give it up."

I tell her about Sheldon's daughter, men with guns.

"What about your friend?" I ask. "Did he get a gun?" Her friend with the unstable employee he decided to let go. Stalks his old boss now. Parks outside the house. One imagines a predictable and terrifying denouement.

"I think he did."

We shut off the lights and lie there. I don't ask for it, the image just pops into my head, those patches of road between here and Atlanta where the deer were struck by cars, smears of red on the pavement, huge and obscene, some of them across two or three lanes. So many as to be almost ordinary.

I hear this thumping behind me. I'm driving home from work the next day. Traffic is slow from months of road repair. In every car you can see the strain; people's expressions range from despair to berserk. Now this noise. In my mirror I see a fluorescent purple Firebird with odd bluish headlights that remind me of zombie eyes. The driver muscles into the left lane, pulls alongside me. He looks over at me, stabbing the air with scissor fingers. He singing, he's having a helluva good time, and my whole car is vibrating. I hate this. While I watch, he guns his engine, surges ahead, then stops.

We sit like this for a full minute. I can see his shoulders bouncing up and down. The music throbs. I'll bet anything he's turned the volume up. From the car in front of me, I see an arm extend through an open window, the driver's palm raised in supplication. The guy must be asking him to please turn the goddamn music down. Scissor fingers reach through the passenger window of the Firebird, form a fist, then the middle finger unfolds in response. The driver in front of me responds in kind.

The next thing I know, the Firebird driver hops out of his car. He's wearing camouflage pants and a sleeveless T-shirt that reveal long tattooed arms. He stomps around the front of his car, reaches inside the car in front of me with his left hand, pulls back and smashes the driver with his right fist. Firebird holds him like that, yelling and swaying to the concussion of bass and drum. It's like he thinks he's in a video. He's enjoying himself. I'm waiting for traffic to move, thinking he'll have to get back in his car. I'm also waiting for someone to do something, when he pulls back his right first again.

What the hell. I'll do what I can.

I honk my horn.

I don't beep it. I lay my forearm across it and mash it.

The Firebird driver pulls his punch, turns to give me a look: You want some of this? He releases the other guy and smiles. I know I'm in trouble, but I'm not giving in. I lay on my horn. Then the car beside me honks. Then the one on the other side of that guy honks. In a few seconds, seven, maybe ten drivers are blasting this guy. He stands there. The dance has gone out of him. More cars honk as he stomps back around the front of his car, gets in, and slams the door.

Traffic begins to inch forward. We're still honking. Everyone has had enough. The drivers in front of him seem to hold back, blocking him. More horns. We're letting him have it, and he can't get away. We all go a little faster, pressing on him.

I realize, wherever this is going, it won't be good. I let up on my horn. I don't want any more. I'd like to get away, but I'm trapped in traffic just the same as he is. We begin to accelerate, a convoy of rage, speeding toward a resolution that we don't deserve and that will solve nothing.

21 / Smitty

Recently the sliding glass doors at Kroger have developed a laugh. Something's amiss with the rollers in one door. It's a female laugh that reminds me of an old aunt. I like to linger in the doorway, clutching my grocery bags, and wait for people to come and go. "You hear that?" I say, inviting strangers into the aura of Aunt Betty's presence. Most people will give a door the time of day. We stand and listen. There's embarrassed mirth. If I were Kroger, I'd have a laughing door at every store.

Today I'm saving the doors for the end of the day. It's 9:00 a.m., and I'm going into the office for a conference with a student. He's been over-exercising the copy-and-paste function on his computer. He's got stubby, transparent chin whiskers and red, allergic eyes. He misses class on account of car trouble and dying grandmas. When he writes sometimes he sounds suspiciously like the *Atlantic Monthly*. Except, of course, when he doesn't, which is most of the time.

I tell students up front, three strikes and you know what. I like him, but it's Richie's third strike. Today he gets an F, for the semester. I feel duty-bound to hand down this verdict in person. "Make this a teachable moment," my colleague Lillian says. "Kick him in the balls." He says he's coming in at noon. When he does, I'll lay out my case—his work, the publications he copied from, the syllabus—then wait for him to see what he's done, and what I have to do.

On the way into the office, I stop and pick up this hitchhiker. It's raining a little. He's at 7 Mile and Telegraph, not a great area, and he's in a wheelchair, a late middle-aged guy, kind of like me, with long gray once-I-was-a-hippie hair, kind of not like me. He's sitting on the side of the road, a suitcase in his lap, facing traffic. The look on his face is determined and pissed off. Go ahead, the face says, pick me up. I pull over and give my horn a tap. I pop the trunk and jump out.

"Where you going?" I ask. I toss his suitcase in the trunk.

"Airport."

"No kidding?" I say.

He rolls over, jerks the passenger door open, starts to climb in. "What," he says, "you think I can't fly?"

This isn't the first time I've seen this guy by the side of the road. A few years ago, same guy, same place, different car. I drove past and sort of did a double take. All right, I gaped at him, and he saw me. He flipped me the bird. I could see words forming on his lips.

"Where you going?" he says now.

"Airport," I say. No eye contact.

"No kidding," he says.

I tell him I'll take him there; it's a crappy day, and I have time. As we merge with traffic, he passes a hand over his hair, which is wet from the rain, then taps his jacket pocket and takes out a cigarette pack. I'm happy to see it's empty. He shakes his head and says, "You probably wouldn't let me smoke anyway."

"Hard being a smoker these days," I say.

Down Telegraph there's one machine shop after another, relieved by fast-food joints and, past a strip of grass on the shoulder, chain-link fences and the backs of garages. A sleety, sooty rain pecks at the windshield.

"This car," he says without looking at me, "has an insipid horn." It's a snotty remark, but I'm pleased he says "insipid." And he's right. I've given up on having an adult car with one of those symphonic horns.

Without asking, he pokes at the radio dial, and the chorus of Madonna's "Material Girl" comes on, loud.

"What's your name?" I yell over the music.

He's nodding in time to the music and doing this thing with his hands, like dancing with his hands, very graceful. "Delbert," he says.

"That's good," I say to him, nodding at his hands. "That's cool."

He tells me he used to crew for Meat Loaf. "Way back in the *Bat out of Hell* days."

"Meat Loaf lived in my hometown for a while," I say. I want to tell him I was in a wheelchair once, too, after getting creamed in a car accident, but I'm afraid he'll find it patronizing. Delbert's doing his hand dance.

"You see him on TV?" he says, "Meat Loaf with Gary Busey? What a nut case."

Which one? I say. Delbert likes this.

"This song reminds me of my kids," I say.

"Madonna is a bitch." Stabbing the radio button again, shutting off the music, he says, "That Malawi thing?"

We stop at a light. "My daughter was just in Malawi," I say.

He turns and squints at me. "What the fuck," he says.

So now we've got Meat Loaf and Malawi to talk about. And wheelchairs.

"Doing what?"

Sightseeing, I'm sure, is the wrong answer. "A friend of hers," I say, "works for this CBO."

"Orphanage?"

Not exactly, I say.

"Probably the same goddamn place. Millions of dollars Madonna drops in Africa. Why doesn't she sprinkle some cash on Detroit?" He taps his cigarette pocket again. "I'll tell you why," he says. "It's not sexy. Who gives a damn about starving kids in Detroit? You wanna be on the cover of *People* magazine?"

I'm picturing my daughter's JPEGs of little Malawian kids. I tell him the kids are cute.

"They're cute in Detroit," he says. Then: "Turn right at the Petco. You mind?"

I kind of mind.

"Time's your flight?" I ask.

"We got time," he says. We swing into a residential area, past two- and three-bedroom ranches, a couple with colored Easter eggs hanging from trees. "I need to stop at my mother's," he says. "Another couple blocks on the right."

The house we stop at is a clone of all the rest. Brown brick ranch, detached garage around the side. This one has a blue Mercury parked out front. "I knew it," Delbert says. There's ramp access to the front porch. To the right of the front door a blue recycling bin is tipped over; to the left a white plastic bag of potting soil is torn open, a dead rose bush sticking out of it. I get his chair out of the trunk, set the brakes on the chair just like I used to. He flops into it. "I'll just be a minute," he says.

I was nineteen when I rode the chair; four months, two broken legs. It was fall. To get me out of the house, my parents did a road trip down the Blue Ridge Parkway, a color tour, where we stayed in one Holiday Inn after another. This was before wheelchair access was invented. My father had moved a lot of furnaces and refrigerators. He knew how to bounce me in and out of hotels, restaurants, visitor centers. Wherever we went I got the look, poor kid in a wheelchair, to which I wanted to say, This is only temporary. This is not me.

I've waited ten minutes in the car and figure that's enough. I hop out of the car, jog up the ramp, and bang on the door a couple times. I can hear yelling. A little man opens the door. He must be eighty or so, balding with saggy cheeks, kind of a potato nose, and sad eyes. I step inside and see Delbert in the living room, his back to the door, leaning forward in his wheelchair, his shirt pulled up exposing his back and shoulders. His skin is the color of oatmeal. He has a burning cigarette clamped between his teeth. The woman who must be his mother is fumbling in her lap with a cardboard package.

"I want him outta here, ma."

"I know you do," she says, "and I just don't care." She's wearing a blue house dress and reminds me of one of those eggs hanging from her neighbors' trees. She picks up her own cigarette, takes a long drag on it, inhales, and blows smoke at the ceiling. "Gracious," she says. Then to me: "You must be Smitty," she says. "Delbert thinks Warren is a smoothy."

Warren shrugs and gives me a regretful smile, as if to say it's hard being a playboy.

"I'm warning you, Warren," Delbert says.

His mother shushes him and applies a patch to each of his shoulders. "You think two'll be enough?" she says.

Delbert squirms back into his shirt, then pulls on his jacket. She hands him the package, which he jams in a bag on the side of his chair. "I want him out of here," he says. "I'm going to have Smitty come by and check. And I don't mean once." He glares at Warren. "Trust me, Warren. You do not want to have Smitty come down on you."

Warren shoots me an alarmed look, tells Delbert to take it easy, he was just leaving.

"You are a good son," the mother says. "If you could just lighten up a little," she adds. She leans forward and Delbert loops his arms around her neck. They hold on that way for longer than I expect.

Warren leaves, then us. Back on Telegraph I say, "Did you tell them I was Smitty?"

"I did not tell them that. I told them about Smitty."

"Did you see Warren? He thought I was Smitty."

"Warren has been sniffing around for months, doing little odd jobs for my mother. For pay. He's stealing from her is what he's doing, and I'm supposed to just let him?" He taps his pocket, pulls out a fresh pack of cigarettes. "Till I got hurt, I did the work. Then I fell off the roof putting up her radar dish. Broke my back."

"You were right," I say.

"Goddamn right I was right."

"No, you were right about my not wanting you to smoke in my car."

He shakes his head and says, "I got a long flight ahead of me. All the way to Amsterdam, and I got little faith in patches to get me through it."

"I'm asking," I say.

"Nice."

"Yes, I'm asking, nicely. Your choice. Another mile and I can drop you off at 1-94."

He turns the pack over in his hands. "You wouldn't."

"You can have a cigarette while you thumb another ride." He's got one in his mouth. "Or you can wait ten minutes and smoke at the airport."

"There's no smoking at the airport."

"And there's no smoking in my car."

"You'd seriously put me out of your car, in the rain," he says, "just because of a cigarette?"

Would I? "It quit raining," I say.

He tucks the cigarette above his ear. "Fuck, man, I could get a ride in two minutes. People are nice."

Out on 1-94, I ask him what's in Amsterdam. Friends, he says. Hash. A change of scenery. As we get closer to the airport, long Delta carriers pass over us, low; first they're quiet, then comes the roar. Delbert gazes up at them. "I figure I'm probably not coming back," he says. Which explains the visit. Which explains the long goodbye hug. "Maybe I can get an operation over there."

At departures drop-off, he thanks for me for the ride. I roll his chair around, lock the wheels. He executes the awkward hang-and-slide maneuver, settles in his chair, retrieves the cigarette from above his ear and lights up. I hand him his suitcase, which he hugs to his lap with his free arm. I tell him to have a good trip and not to worry.

"Warren looks like a nice guy," I say.

"Smitty'll take care of Warren," he says. "Trust me, he'll put the fear of death in him." He gives the door a shove and swings his chair around, pointed toward the terminal.

"Hey," he says, looking around, exhaling a puff of smoke, "somebody wanna give me a shove?"

I call in for messages as I'm pulling away from the airport. There's one from Richie. "Um, I can't come in today," he says. "But I know what I done." There's a pause. He turns away from the phone and says something, probably to one of his grandmas. "I know what I *did*," he says, "and I know that you have to fail me for it, but I just wanted you to know I learned a ton in your class, and I was wondering if I could come in tomorrow and talk to you anyway." He says he's learned his lesson. He asks me for just one more chance and leaves me his number. I suppose Lillian would kick him in the balls over the phone.

When I stop at the Kroger that afternoon, there's a woman standing outside with her back to the laughing doors. She's all dressed up in black pants and jacket, with her silver hair elegantly done. It looks like she's waiting for a limo.

"Are they laughing today?" I ask her.

She looks at me, draws herself up, and says, "What? Who?"

"The doors."

Just then they slide open, and a gentleman, also dressed in black, walks out, takes her arm. She looks at me and smiles.

The doors roll shut with Aunt Betty's laugh sounding better than ever. I know it won't last. Kroger will eventually fix the doors. I wait for a few more laughs, a sound I figure I can use almost as much as the occasional fear of death.

22 / Still Alive

The day is too gorgeous for something like this to happen. At 11:00 a.m. I'm northbound on Telegraph Road when, ahead of me on the left, in a rush of brown, a dog runs onto the road and is struck by a silver Lexus. The animal goes airborne and comes down in the middle of the road. It tries to get up. Its rear legs peddle, driving the creature around in circles, as if it's pinned to the road.

Then I see it's not a dog. It's a fawn.

In the car next to mine, a woman turns and gapes at me, as if to say, Do something. What should we do? I pull to the shoulder and get out of my car. It's a warm October day, golden. The animal spins, frantic, its wide black eyes terrified. The stream of traffic slows, then begins to flow around the deer. The Lexus is long gone. Another driver stops. He gets out of his car. "We can't help," he says. "It would be dangerous to try to move it."

I take out my phone and call 911.

"So you just left?" my wife says. We're lying in bed that night.

"An injured deer is dangerous," I say.

"A fawn? How you could just leave?"

"There was nothing to do." I wonder who 911 sent. A cop. He secured the scene. He assessed the deer from afar, how close to death, how much danger to traffic. He approached, took out his service weapon. Would that happen?

"I wonder where the mother was," she says.

Maybe there's a kit, like an AED, that they take with them in these emergencies, with directions. How to decease a deer.

"Where were you going," she says, "that you couldn't wait?"

"It was really terrible," I say.

She turns a page in her book, shakes her head in disgust. From the attic, over our heads, comes a ticking sound we've heard for a few days. I'll have to go up there, but not tonight.

"To the gym," I say.

Three days a week I go to the local senior center to exercise. On the ground floor is Scrabble, jigsaw puzzles, a few meeting rooms for cultural enrichment events, and the launchpad for meals on wheels. Downstairs is a gym. The major seniors prefer the pneumatic weight machines; chat-friendly, sitting required. Minor seniors walk the treadmills and the indoor track. I think of myself as neither. I'm more like an apprentice senior. I run. I rev up the elliptical. On a good day my rate of exercise inspires shock and awe.

The day after the deer incident I'm on a treadmill watching two TVs, *Good Morning America* and the *Today Show*. There are three stories today. Chilean miners emerging from that rescue canister, *Dancing with the Stars*, and celebrity cougars jilted by their young studs. The major seniors ignore all this. A minor senior taps me on the shoulder. He points to the TV. "You mind if I change channel?" On the screen in front of us, Ashton Kutcher is explaining what happened to him and Demi Moore.

The minor senior is wearing khaki shorts and a University of Arizona T-shirt. On the tag clipped to his belt I see he's number ten. We're all tagged at check-in, I suppose in case we drop dead, they know who to call.

"Fine," I say.

He thumbs the remote to a financial channel on one TV. Graphs of stock futures appear on screen. On the other screen I see Courteney Cox with what's his name, also unfaithful. I'm wondering what happened to the fawn. I'm also thinking about the sound I've been hearing at night, in the attic. Years ago, a friend's attic was full of bats.

That afternoon I call a pest service. I talk to Amanda. "Ticking?" she says.

"Louder than that," I say.

"Fluttering?"

I tell her I can't be sure, but something's up there. She wonders if I hear the sound during the day. "I'm not sure. Do you think it's bats?"

"Go listen."

"Right now?"

She says it would help, before she sends someone out, to have a more detailed sonic profile. A service call is $100.

"Does that sound like a flutter?" I ask my wife that night. She's reading a novel about the grandson of Zoroaster. The thing in the attic is acting up. My wife is still upset about the deer. "Fawn," she says. "Stop saying *deer*."

When I was in high school, I tell her, there was a local monster myth, a thing called deer man. We went looking for it, or him, on weekend nights.

"It's not a flutter," she says. "Whatever it is, it better not die up there."

The next morning, the minor senior in khakis asks me again about changing the channel. His program is called *Squawk Box*. When it's been on a few minutes, I pull out my earbuds and tell him one of the talking heads looks like Dos Equis man. He gives me an impatient look, then takes off his headset. "The Dos Equis man," I say, "the most interesting man in the world?" He shakes his head, perturbed. I decide against explaining. It's not worth it. If he can't mix money and mirth, he'll be in trouble someday. I press my earbuds back in and step on it.

My first time on the elliptical, the trainer tapped me on the shoulder to tell me I was going backward. "It's okay," she said. "I just thought you'd like to know."

Backward. Half the music on my iPod is forty years old. The major seniors in front of me remind me of what lies ahead. In this game, progress is remembering your former self, forestalling what's next.

That afternoon I go out to the garage, look for my son's old catcher's mask. If it's bats, I figure I'll need protection. I heard somewhere that bats, if they attack, go for your eyes. Or maybe it was your hair. I pull on the mask, then think, no, a determined bat could easily penetrate that defense. I go back in the house, open a cupboard, and take out his swim goggles. I get them on and catch my reflection in a window. Foolish. In the end, I settle on a tennis racket.

In the upstairs hallway, I open the stepladder, climb up, and take out the four screws holding the attic fan in place. Then I lift the fan, rotate it, and slide it out of the way, leaving space to crawl up there. I climb back down, get my tennis racket, and ascend into that stuffy, shadowy space. Up there I can I hear kids across the street yelling. I half expect to find bats hanging from the rafters, grinning at me with their upside-down faces. I stand there a few minutes looking, listening. Somewhere, the former owner of the house is wondering what happened to the family board games. Sorry, Monopoly, Risk, Stratego, they lie there on a bed of insulation.

I'm looking for floor joists to walk on when the tapping sound starts up, only it's not tapping, it's flapping, quick and close, so close to my head I step back and almost fall on the fan. More fluttering around my head. It freaks me out, but I am determined. I follow the sound, turning my head. Then it stops. Up there, clinging to the side of the chimney, I see, it's a grackle. It holds a few seconds, then launches, doing laps around the attic now that I've startled it.

I wonder if there's a nonviolent way to stop a bird in flight with a tennis racket. The bird will have to come to me, because if I go to it and step wrong, I'll put my foot through the ceiling of my house. Just then the bird stops again on the chimney, right next to me, clutching the bricks with its bird claws, its whole body heaving.

I backhand it, gently smashing it against the brick with the racket.

It's alive, terrified with its whole body, which I manage to grasp and hold in my hand. I feel it trembling as I climb down the ladder. I'm afraid it will pee on me. Frogs, I know, pee. So I'm in a hurry to get outside and let it go. In my hand, right up my arm, I feel its terrible fear, its crushing sense of doom, and it's so awful, I can't wait to get rid of it. It's like holding a bomb.

I push through the front door and set the grackle down at the edge of the driveway. Nothing. I nudge it with my foot. It doesn't move. I wonder if it died of fright, if its heart exploded. "Go on," I say to it. Rolled on its side, it looks pretty dead.

I go back in the house, climb up in the attic to retrieve my tennis racket. The games I decide to just leave up there, for the next owner. After replacing the attic fan and folding the ladder shut, I come down the stairs and walk out through the garage. I check the edge of the drive. No grackle.

Next day, before going to the senior center, I take the same drive up Telegraph Road, stopping at the township offices. I ask for the 911 dispatcher and am directed down the hall, where I meet Officer Kane. I ask about the fawn called in a few days ago, does she know what happened. She clicks her computer mouse. Data flows across her face. "It was gone," she says, "by the time we got there." Half the time when they make a deer run, she explains, the animal has already been picked up.

"Deer guys," she says, "in pickup trucks."

"What if it was still alive?" I ask.

She shrugs. "Deer guys know what to do."

I'm thinking about the fawn, tossed in the back of a truck, when I check in at the senior center a few minutes later. It's a light day, most of the machines quiet. My minor senior friend is watching *Squawk Box*. He looks full of hope. A few major seniors are seated, preparing to exert themselves. The woman at check-in takes my ID, hands me my tag. "You're nineteen today," she says.

I look at the tag. It's purple, the number printed in large black font. I clip it to my shirt.

"Nineteen," I say.

"What's new with you?"

"Not much." I think about telling her that I saved a bird's life yesterday, that I held it in my bare hands, and just what that felt like. I decide against it and head for the elliptical next to my friend.

He smiles, asks me how I'm doing.

Still alive, I tell him. That's a start.

23 / Badass

"Feel my face," I say to my wife.

It's a Saturday morning in August. We're on our way to the farmers' market—not our usual farmers' market, where we know whose tomatoes we want, whose zucchini are the size we like. It's a new market. She wants to see if Toby, our peach man, is there, or that failing, maybe we can find a substitute Toby.

"Why would he be there?" I ask.

"He might be," she says. "There's a chance."

"Feel it," I say. "I shaved."

"I see that."

I seriously doubt she sees it. But I'll take it. She reaches over, rubs my jaw with the back of her hand. "Soft as a baby's ass," she says.

I know she worries about Toby. A couple winters ago, he lost all his peach trees.

"It's his livelihood," she says. "What's the poor guy going to do?"

The weather here warmed up in February, then froze hard again in March. We thought the cold killed his trees, but evidently it was steady, slashing wind that did them in. For years, from mid-July to mid-September, he brought free-stone peaches to market. Approaching his stand, you heard his booming voice and his easy laugh. Leaning over his tables, a billcap yanked down over his wild hair, he smiled through a full unruly red beard, refilling half-peck boxes with peaches from bushel baskets piled in the back of his rusted Chevy van.

"These are Red Havens," he'd say. "Wait a few days before you eat them."

Another day, "These are my Lucky 13s. They're almost ready."

The fruit came in steady and sweet over the last weeks of summer, PF 17S, PF 23S, PF 27S. One year he announced a new variety that he called his mutants. (When asked, he provided no explanation.) They were a revelation. Try one, he'd say. And we would. We trusted him. He had the rumpled look of an almost homeless guy. Word around the market was he arrived on site in the early hours, slept in his truck, and woke up still drunk. All that. And amazing peaches.

Those summers, almost every day at lunch and dinner we peeled and sliced a half a dozen Tobys into bowls of red wine for dessert. Peeled, his peaches were shiny, brilliant gold. They took on mythic status at our table. You could imagine a Renaissance painting, *Madonna and Child Holding a Peach*, with one of Toby's peeled golden orbs in the Christ child's hand, a beatific look on his face.

You would have to imagine that, because as far as I can tell, the poor kid never got peaches. You can find blasé baby Jesuses eating grapes, toddler Jesus deciding to try a fig, a beautifully coiffed Jesus holding a pear and rolling his eyes (as if he's thinking *this again?*), Botticelli Jesus eating a pomegranate, a bored look on his face, waving at the fruit vendor (*Don't you have any peaches, man?*). And always and everywhere, it's apples, apples, and more apples.

The apple, of course, is an essential prop in biblical human history; also probably a mistake. Given regional geographic and horticultural facts, it's unlikely there was a single apple tree in the Garden of Eden. Eve probably plucked and ate an ethrog or a quince or a date. But in Latin, the word for apple and evil are the same. Thanks to the Church of Rome, that's Adam and Eve's fruit of choice. If it was good enough for them, it was good enough for Jesus.

A boring fruit, my wife maintains.

Baby Jesus, I think, would agree. When you see him in some paintings, he does not look like a happy baby. One of Toby's mutants could have made his day.

I pass a hand over my cheek, where my wife's hand just traveled. It was a perfunctory shave this morning, because, unlike Toby, and unlike grown-up Jesus, I am not a beardful man.

I shave today much the same as I did when I was a kid. In fact, I started shaving with an old Norelco electric my father had retired. Maybe he didn't trust me with a razor. The shaver had a blue travel case with a busted zipper. It also came with a little brush for brooming whiskers out of the well beneath the rotors, which I needed to do on a semiannual basis. It was this shaver that I took to college with me, storing it in the dank, filmy dorm bathroom, where my roommates kept their accessories: razors, cans of shaving soap, aftershave lotions. I'd get up most mornings, look in the mirror, and think, No, not today.

Lots of guys on campus had beards. It's what guys do, right? The first girl I went out with in college, on our second date, at some point in the evening saw my face in just the right slant of light. She asked me, "Did you shave?"

I sensed this was a trick question. "Yes?"

She smiled and pointed. "You missed a couple spots."

It was easy to do, given that my facial hair was, and still is, mostly transparent.

I transitioned to an actual razor around this time—a decision requiring a few manly decisions. Somewhere I had heard that shaving with a razor *caused* your beard to grow. It was a stimulus-response bet worth a try. I went with a Schick razor that you shucked refill blades into, rather the way I imagined chambering a bullet in a gun. On a round black knob on the handle end of the razor was a black ball with four-speed shift legend on it, an adolescent touch, I admit. I went through a series of shaving soaps, foams, creams, gels, and butters, looking for the one that both gave me a close shave and supposedly called forth a thicker, lustier beard. I knew from TV that some products were better than others at softening a man's beard, not really a factor in my case. The whole ritual was imbued with equal parts hope and farce. For me, a razor was little more than a squeegee.

In his new book *Of Beards and Men*, Christopher Oldstone-Moore argues that, throughout history, from Alexander the Great forward, shaving was pretty much the norm. Oldstone-Moore identifies four main periods in Western history when beards were a big deal: during the time of the Emperor Hadrian, in the Middle Ages and the Renaissance, and the nineteenth century (see Walt Whitman). For Hadrian, influenced by the Stoics, shaving was about being natural: "[The importance of nature] is very explicit in the first beard movement, because Hadrian was following the teachings of Stoic philosophy. The Stoics were explicitly—in fact all the philosophers—were in favor of beards as a sign of following the rule of nature."

There was, I think, a similar sense when I was coming of age. In the late sixties, when guys tuned in, turned on, and dropped out, in their efforts to get back to nature, facial hair was definitely on the syllabus. Some of my friends grew their hair and their beards; when they did so, more than a few were derided by their fathers for trying to be Jesus look-alikes. By the mid-1970s I finally achieved significant hair on my head. By then, however, I was also more or less resigned to the fact that great facial hair was not in the cards.

Over the next few decades I flirted a few times with the idea of growing a beard. Sometime in the nineties, a friend and I went on a ski trip together.

"Let's grow beards," he said. In my heart I knew: he might as well have suggested I fly the plane. But I thought, Maybe now is the time. I had sired two children. My growth, while patchy and still transparent, had definitely thickened in places. Maybe I had a beard in me.

We booked a Thursday night flight to Salt Lake City. I quit shaving the Monday before that (which meant I already had two to three days' "growth"). I felt a little sheepish about it. It was like starting the race before the starting gun was fired, but what the hell.

"Well?" he said as we buckled in for takeoff. He said his last shave was that morning.

I found a minor patch of grizzle on my face, scratched it, and shrugged. "Why are we doing this?"

"Come on," he said, "you got it going." I swear he was squinting to see it when he said that.

You feel ridiculous. The flight attendant who checked to see if I was buckled—did I detect a smirk? The guy selling lift tickets at the ski area, a Jeremiah Johnson look-alike—was he ruffling his beard to draw ironic attention to my face? On the gondola, in the bar, standing in front of a urinal, everywhere I went, I asked myself, Am I really putting my best face forward?

Never mind it didn't look convincing. It didn't feel good. My face was irritated. It felt like it was breaking out, like my face had a low-level fever. Men with beards love their faces. They rub their beards, they fondle them in public. I didn't want to do that. I just wanted to get rid of it. Saturday evening, after our second full day of skiing, after some five to seven full days of hard work, I turned on all the lights in the bathroom and examined my beard. I had more hair in my ears than on my chin. It wasn't happening. I peeled the wrapper off a fresh bar of complimentary soap, lathered up, and shaved.

Oldstone-Moore observes, "Right back to the beginning of civilization you see people thinking that the removal of hair is a kind of purification, the removal of the animal self." It was a relief. I got back to my human self. It wasn't so much animal as *clown* self I had removed.

Beardlessness equates with youth. That's a bad thing? In ancient times athletes shaved their beards, in some cases shaved their bodies, to appear young, to show off their muscles. I remember my shock a few years ago, during a World Series, at the number of bearded baseball players there were. It seemed incongruous, indecorous, even a little barbarous. To this day, the New York Yankees have maintained their no-beards rule.

Not long ago my son, now thirty-three, texted me a selfie, a *bearded* selfie. He lives in Los Angeles. Weather permitting, he rides a skateboard to the ad agency where he works. In times of need, he has given me fashion advice.

We have a similar facial structure, similar gaps in beard growth. Or so I thought. His beard had filled in pretty well. Hardly any gaps. And oddly, it looked reddish.

"Wow," I texted back.

"Yeah."

"Did you color it?"

"A little."

"Does she like it?" The girlfriend, that is.

"Yes. She says I touch my face too much."

"That happens."

I show my wife the photo, tell her I might want to try again. Wouldn't she like a man with a little scruff? I'm joking, but not 100 percent. Just once, I would like to see my face with hair on it. I'd be happy with medium stubble.

I show her the photo a second time.

"Dreadful," she says.

"I was thinking . . ."

"No," she says.

"Aren't you at all curious?"

"If I wanted a man with a beard," my wife says, "I would have married one."

I would need to go into the wilderness. What could I accomplish in forty days? Not much. It might take years to make visible my inner wild man.

On the way home from the market, we stop at a Lebanese restaurant. We found good Michigan peaches. No Toby. I would like to think the peaches we bought are mutants. We order shawarma and *kafta* from a server with soft black flowing facial hair. Maybe he's twenty.

I can't help myself. "Quite a beard," I say.

He nods and smiles.

I ask how long it took to grow.

"It's been a few weeks now," he says.

My wife looks at me across the table, shakes her head.

"Badass," he says. "Don't you think?"

Many things. Among them, most certainly, badass.

24 / Stand Up

"Why don't the trees fall down?"

I was pulling out of the local elementary school, where I'd just dropped off my daughter, a third-grader. It was 8:35 a.m., a sunny day. Seated in the back seat of the car, my preschool-bound son was looking out the car windows. At that age, belted into the back seat of a car, about all you can see outside is trees. It was late spring. The trees weren't just leafing out. They were practically gushing green.

"Trees just stand up," I said. "That's what makes them trees."

He took a thoughtful suck on his thumb and considered my answer. "Don't they get tired?"

I took a thoughtful sip of coffee, considering his question. "What if they all decided to lie down and take a rest?"

A little more thumb.

I caught his face in the rearview mirror. He was gazing out the car windows, making it work. "Like spaghetti," he said. He smiled, satisfied with his science. "But we'd want them to stand up again."

Right now I'm trying to fix a few bent-over trees at the edge of our yard. Between our house and the neighbors' is a clump of cedars. They've stopped standing up. They have felt the weight of snow and ice, and lost their will to be trees.

One of the things I took from my father's workshop after he died was rope. He had a lot of it, nylon and hemp, coiled and hanked, knotted and loose. I took it all, without thinking much about the symbolism. I just thought I'd need it sometime. I also took what he called a coffin hoist, a come-along ratchet winch. I'm using these tools to make the trees stand up.

Technically, these are the neighbors' trees. My wife's position is that Jed, the neighbor, should just cut these failed cedars down. For her, this is an astonishing assertion. She loves trees with a fierceness that makes me jealous. She mourned the loss of a craggy ant-infested apple tree when we cut it down some time ago. For a few years now she has been saying goodbye, limb by scabrous limb, to the sepulchral mountain ash in our front yard. When she sees new maples squirting out of the flowerbeds, with trunks no bigger than skewers, she sees future trees. She delights in the sound of wind in their future leaves, she basks in their future shade. But the cedars, to her, are as good as dead.

"I'd like to screw an eye into that tree," Jed says to me one day. We're standing at the edge of my driveway.

I smile at the linguistic strangeness of this statement (he means an eye*bolt*), then tell him no, that would be impossible.

"Then we could pull those cedars upright," he says.

That we could pull those trees upright, by hand, and tie them off, I seriously doubt.

But the more important sticking point is the tree in question, the anchor tree, a large cottonwood nearly three feet in diameter, nine feet in circumference, a viable tree close enough to our driveway to be ours. (We pay to have it trimmed. Maintenance, I figure, is 95 percent of possession.) It is, in truth, a miserable plant. It drops a gazillion seedpods—they resemble goose droppings—in early spring, from which seeds emerge. These seeds are the size of almonds. They emit a sticky sap that glues them to your shoes, stains a car's paint job, and leaves brown gluey curlicues on a windshield. Then there's the cotton, flurries of the stuff, that can last a month. And then there's the sticks a cottonwood tree sheds in abundance, year around. Still, my wife loves this tree. To screw an eye into it would be to inflict bodily harm upon it and possibly let death in. She will have none of it.

Jed and I table the measure, or so I think.

A few days later I look out and see his stepladder leaning against our tree, and five or six wraps of white three-quarter-inch nylon rope around the trunk, at eye level. He's proceeding with the fix.

"It's an eyesore," my wife says.

"It's a compromise." I tell her about the eyebolt, and she gets a little ballistic. To me, no bolt was a neighborly concession on Jed's part. But the white rope, there is no denying it, is ugly.

My wife says, "He does these things just to make me angry."

"I don't think so."

A week goes by. It's full spring. Our driveway is covered with brown cottonwood pods. It looks like it's been raining turds. And the stepladder is still there. And the rope, wrapped around our cottonwood, disappearing ineffectually into the little grove of decrepit cedars.

My wife decides the trees must die.

"He just wants them to straighten up," I say. "Wouldn't you? You love trees."

"He should cut them down. They'll never stand up again."

In physics, what little I had, in the section on strength of materials, I learned about fatigue. Over time, repeated loads on a material cause stress. Materials have a stress limit. Exceed that limit and fatigue occurs—cracks, loss of tensile strength. Fatigue is permanent. Materials do not recover from fatigue, even when rested. Think of a rubber band that's lost its *boing*.

"Why do you care, anyway?" she asks.

She is more of a friend to trees than I am. I mow around them. I rake up their droppings. I clean up after the cottonwood. Why do I care?

Because I don't want to look over there and see nothing.

Because I want them to stand up.

Also, at the risk of getting psychological about it, maybe a short person values tall things, reacts with a natural sense of awe. I am short. And it's difficult for a man, particularly a young man, to be short; possibly more difficult than for a woman, particularly a young woman, to be tall.

These past weeks I've noticed the posture of a woman in one of my classes. Trudy is my best student. Whatever I suggest she try, she does, and quickly masters. In her writing there is energy, invention, clarity, and wit. Every day she walks into class, I notice how she carries herself. Trudy has tall-girl hunch. I also notice her reserve, such diffidence in this capable person. She's more than shy. I wonder what happened. One day she says she has a twin. I picture these two women together, Trudy and Judy walking side by side, making themselves smaller on purpose. Another day, during a conference, I ask her what her plan is. She smiles and lowers her head. It is then I notice the tiny shiny silver dot in her cheek, a piercing. She says she wants to be an art teacher. I tell her she will be a marvelous teacher, and she will be.

But what I want to say is: "Trudy, be full size."

A few days pass. I decide to address the trees.

At Joann Fabrics I buy a length of nylon webbing, like the safety strap on a car seat, like the shoulder strap on Trudy's backpack. It's an inch in diameter, ten feet long. Gray would match cottonwood bark. Joann's does not have gray. I settle for black. At Home Depot I buy a metal ring and an eye swivel. Back home, a few pop rivets properly administered, and I have a strap, which I wrap around the cottonwood. I attach the coffin hoist to Jed's three-quarter-inch white nylon rope and get to work, pulling a bent cedar upright. I tie the tree off with one-quarter-inch nylon rope, black; then I do the next tree, then the next. In the end, five crosshatching black lines, barely visible, hold the cedars upright. It might work.

I coil Jed's rope the way my father taught me and lay it at the edge of the lot.

If she notices my work, my wife doesn't acknowledge it. The trees, she thinks, are doomed. It's only a matter of time.

We'll see. They are fatigued. But they are also living things. Maybe they will recover and stand up straight, be fully themselves. That's what I want.

25 / Waterful

"It looks funny."

"Not all the time," I say.

My daughter is addressing my head. We're in the kitchen on a Sunday morning. I've been shelling fava beans and enjoying the hum coming from the basement, where our Frigidaire dehumidifier is keeping us dry. We had water down there a while ago, a crisis. Today the sun is out, and these fava, shucked and blanched and removed from their little jackets, are brilliant green. They will make a fine pasta sauce. She levels her index finger at my ear, making a little statement. I'm getting the point. That I have a fresh haircut, that something's not quite right in the ear zones.

"It's the straight edge." She holds a hand next to her right ear, makes a sawing motion. "It looks chopped."

I tell her a new guy is cutting my hair.

"Chopped."

"She's right," my wife says.

So this is a pleasant conversation.

From the kitchen I make a stealth move to the bathroom, turn on the light, and consult the mirror. Some haircuts need a week or two before they look right. This one, for example. While I'm in there, the doorbell rings. Through the bathroom window, I see a head of carefully combed black hair on the front porch.

I pull the front door open to a thin guy, medium height, fortyish. He's wearing a gray jacket. There's a clipboard clamped under his left arm. So he's selling something. On a Sunday morning? From the corner of his mouth, curving down to his chin, he has a thin red scar.

I push the screen door open.

"I'm Alex," he says. "I cleaned your gutters last year."

Alex the Russian gutter man. He came out last spring, when my wife got fed up with my antics during rainstorms.

He hands me his card. It's Aleks. Sounds like Alex. A guy at the hardware store gave me his number.

"I looked," he says. "Your gutters are full. I clean them tomorrow, same price as last year."

We have dirty trees in the yard, a big maple, a bunch of cottonwoods. The gutters and downspouts get clogged. In a hard rain, when water spills from them, I like to toss on a raincoat, hike up a ladder, and clean the downspout blockage. There's a sudden rush of water along the gutter, down the spout. It's instant gratification at its best. But dangerous. According to the Center for Disease Control, ladders account for over one hundred thousand injuries a year—probably many more go unreported—and three hundred deaths. I try to be careful, I try to think with my feet climbing up and down, but sometimes your feet don't pay attention. Please stay off the ladder, my wife says.

Aleks says he'll see me Monday.

Water comes at us, from above and below. One spring, during a prolonged Michigan monsoon, water leaked into our basement, through the floor. Lots of it. We were getting ready to go away. Two consecutive days, fresh out of bed in the morning, I walked down to the basement in my bare feet, pausing on the bottom step. Outside it rained and rained. In the basement, the water rose. It was a calamity.

What do you do?

It's hard not to panic. If you panic, and if you're still a little old school, you take down the Yellow Pages from that shelf in the closet. You pick out some big ads and some little ads. Make a few calls.

The first outfit sent a salesman to give us an estimate. They would bust the floor all the way around the inside perimeter of the basement, install drain tile, gravel, patch the floor. They could fit us into their busy schedule, like, the very next day. The repair would cost $12,000. The second outfit sent a salesman to give us an estimate. The dispatcher said the guy would only come when both my wife and I were home. Why's that? I asked. They just preferred it that way. We'll be home tonight, I said, trying hard not to sound desperate.

When the salesman came through the front door that night, he had two notebooks under his arm. Notebooks that were actually photo albums. How-we-fix-your-basement photos, I assumed. The second album he opened was that. The first photo album he opened, the fatter one, was pictures of basements with mold. Black mold. Gray mold. Speckled mold, splotchy mold. Basements with total mold everywhere. He slid the photo album to the center of the kitchen table and rotated it, aimed ever so slightly in my wife's direction. With the desired effect.

"Oh," she said.

"Mold," he said. "I can't emphasize it enough: you have to move fast on this." He turned a page. More photos, more mold.

She looked at me.

He said, "It happens every time."

He said, "It's probably already gotten a head start on us."

He said, "Do you have allergies?"

"Yes," she said.

"Laundry room is in the basement?"

"Yes," she said.

You are the devil, I thought.

Then he opened the how-we-fix-your-basement book. He talked about the water table (high) and hydrostatic pressure (intense). He said their approach was to bust the floor all the way around the inside perimeter of the basement, install drain tile, gravel, patch the floor. Outside the house they would dig down to the footing, waterproof the basement walls, replace the outside drain tile, freshen the gravel, and backfill. We'd never have water again, guaranteed.

My wife was still looking at the mold.

Total cost of the repair: $24,000.

I said we needed time to think about it. We still had to talk to a few more people. Thanks for coming. He left us a written estimate, reminding us as I was pushing him out the door of the all-important issue, mold.

My wife and I sat at the kitchen table, looking at each other. It was a lot of money. The water down there didn't seem to be going anywhere. We had pulled out carpet, taken it to the road. We had rearranged stuff, getting our valuable basement junk off the wet floor. It was a mess.

In reality, we didn't have a few more people to see. All the ads in the Yellow Pages looked more or less alike. Surely, I said to my wife, there was someone who knew about these things, someone smart, someone we could trust. Then I remembered.

Walter.

Her cousin Walt is in the poured-wall business. He's made basements for people for fifty years. Hundreds of basements. No, thousands of basements. He must have fielded a few water-in-the-basement complaints.

"Yeah, I got a guy," Walt said when I got him on the phone. "He's a genius."

"Good."

"He's a wizard."

"What's his number?"

"He understands water. He just *gets* it."

"What's his number?"

"He'll come," Walt said. "But you gotta bug him."

The guy's name was Ivan Bogner. Walt gave me a phone number, adding that it might not be the right number because Ivan Bogner had to change phones all the time. His cell phone regularly fell out of his pocket and into pools of muddy water. I pictured a basement full of water, a guy in scuba gear, holding an underwater flashlight, diving under basement floors and getting to the source of the problem.

I bugged Ivan Bogner for two days. I left too many messages, apologizing in every one of them for calling again, for needing his help so bad, needing it as soon as he could possibly come, and did I mention that Walt was my wife's cousin?

On the afternoon of the third day, a white van pulled up in front of the house. A little guy, probably in his sixties, climbed out of the vehicle. He was muscular. He wore white painter's pants and a white T-shirt. His hair was cut close to his head. The white van and his white clothes were spotless. He looked like he could be an actor in a TV commercial for Mr. Clean or the Man from Glad. He loped up the driveway, shoved through the open door, and asked me to show him to the basement.

"Block," he said, pointing at the basement walls.

"Right," I said. "It's a cement block basement. Does that matter?"

"No."

I told him the guys we'd talked to so far said we needed all new drain tile.

"Who are they?"

"I found them in the Yellow Pages."

He shook his head. "I'll get my tools."

"Right now?" I thought I should ask, What about an estimate? How much is this going to cost? He was already charging up the stairway.

Ivan Bogner carried in a large power drill and an electric jackhammer. He pointed at the corner of the basement and said he would drill a hole through the wall into the drain tile. He told me he needed garden hose. He drilled. I fetched a hose, one end of which he connected to the laundry tub faucet. The other end he fed through the hole he had drilled in the wall.

"Now," he said, "turn on the water."

We were standing in an inch of water in my basement, and he wanted me to turn on the water. He wanted to introduce more water to an already very bad water situation. It seemed like throwing gasoline on a fire to put it out.

"I need to know if your drain tile is blocked," he said. "Turn on the water."

We let it run three to four minutes.

"Good," he said.

He told me shut it off, pulled out the hose, and said he would patch the hole later.

Using the jackhammer, he broke a ten-inch hole in the concrete floor on one side of the basement, revealing a high muddy lake under the floor. He found exactly what he was looking for: tile leading from the footing to a central tile line that went to the sump hole in the corner of the basement. He broke a hole in the tile. It was full of water.

"Good," he said.

On the other side of the basement, he broke another ten-inch hole in the concrete floor, finding more tile. Also the high muddy lake. He got down on his hands and knees, reaching down into the water.

"Here's the problem," he said. He was dragging his right hand through the water, hauling mud out of the hole. "It's a broken joint in the tile." There was a distinct swooshing sound as water started to flow past the blockage while he scooped more mud from the tile. Water gushed toward the sump hole.

"Your pump is going run for the next few hours." He clawed more muck out of the hole. "Get your dehumidifier going. We'll get you dried out down here. It will take a couple days." He stood up. His whites were muddy. The water rushed gloriously through the tile.

"Those companies you talked to," he said, "what were they going to charge you to fix this problem?"

When I told him, he shook his head in disgust. "Some of those people," he said, "they have no shame."

A few days later he came back, patched the tile and the holes in the wall and floor. When I asked him what we owed him, he said he would send us the bill. He never sent it. I called, I left messages. Then his number went out of service. I got the new number from Walt. Called. No bill. We've been dry ever since.

Ever since Ivan Bogner was here, the first thing I do when I get up in the morning is walk downstairs in my bare feet and empty the dehumidifier tank. Every day it takes two gallons of water out of the air down there, keeping us dry, holding the mold at bay. It could probably do more, according to the manual, it could do as much as seventy pints a day, but for now, for my own peace of mind, I want to be exact. I want to know. Two gallons a day.

Every morning I pour this water down the laundry tub drain. It's sort of a ritual; I feel actively involved.

Lately my wife has been saying we could put that water to use, if I would just carry it upstairs.

And do what with it? I wonder.

Water plants, she says.

Sure, we could do that. Really, I get it. All that water down the drain: it seems like a shameful waste. But really, carry water up the stairs, every day, walking past how many faucets in the process?

Water is heavy, two gallons is almost twenty pounds.

And of course water in Michigan is plentiful. According to United States Geological Services, out of all the fifty states and the District of Columbia, Michigan ranks number one for the amount of surface area covered with water, 41.5 percent. That's 40,175 square miles of surface area: lake, strait, bay, river, stream, spring, brook, creek, crick, ditch, pond, pool, marsh, bog, wetland, swamp. That's a lot of water.

And then there's the Great Lakes.

Still, I get it. Water is a curse and a blessing. It has a power that will have its way with us, a power we can harness. Some years ago, before our water woes, I was talking to a colleague about making use of water running off the roof. I fantasized about capturing water during rainstorms, using it to grow a voluptuous garden in the backyard. He suggested a cistern. And for a day or two, I thought it just might work. Roof, gutters, downspouts, a simple system for transferring and banking water.

Then I wondered: How much water is that?

A lot.

One inch of rainfall on one thousand square feet of roof amounts to 620 gallons of water. Our roof is roughly three times that size. The average yearly rainfall in the Detroit area is thirty-three inches, making for a yearly capture of some sixty-one thousand gallons of rainwater.

What on earth would we do with all that water?

Come Monday Aleks climbs up on the roof. He uses a battery-powered blower to blow leaves and junk off the roof. With a putty knife he scraps all the crud out of the gutters. He's sure-footed up there. And not a hair out of place. I consider asking who cuts his hair, then decide to let it go. I'll give my new guy one more chance.

Aleks works fast. He does a better job than I do.

Later, when I write him the check, he points to all our tree cover, wonders if he should come again in the fall.

By all means, I say, see you in the fall. I tell him I'll pass his name and number to people I know.

Water above, water below, under control.

Some days, during a gentle rain, I stand on the back porch and listen to runoff coursing along the gutters. It has its own distinct music. It's soothing. For the time being, at least, we have the upper hand.

26 / We're Melting

"If we open the house," my wife says, "it will only make things worse."

We're lying in bed one July night. The power is out. No AC. The windows are closed.

"But it's hot," I say.

"We don't want to let the humidity in."

Of course it's humid. This is Michigan. In summer this is the steam bath state. Still, I can't stop thinking about air temperature, which I figure to be at least seven to ten degrees lower outside than inside.

It's been two days since a thunderstorm came through the area, separating limbs from trees, taking down power lines and, with them, our electricity and our AC. These two days we've kept the house sealed shut, curtains pulled. Fine for a day. Day two, it's like occupying a hot cave. The night of day two, upstairs where we sleep, with temperatures in the attic above us well in excess of 100 degrees, the distinction between dry heat and wet heat loses all meaning. Hot is hot.

I ponder cool outdoor air, trying to force from my mind what I know about heating and cooling: heat goes to cold. When you open a window on a cold winter day, you don't let cold in. You let heat out, to be replaced by, what, the absence of heat? This night, if we open a window, if we let the heat out of our bedroom, I picture a long gradual emptying of the house's heat, heat flowing through our room, a lava-flow of heat from the other bedrooms upstairs, heat traveling up the stairway, funneling its way to our room; a river of slow, suffocating heat pouring out of the house, making room, possibly by morning, for the absence of heat.

"Remember the humidity," she says.

I toss back the damp sheet and slide out of bed, telling her I'm going downstairs to sleep on the couch.

"And don't open the windows down there. We need to keep the house closed."

Most humans are at constant war with the natural world. Living in harmony with nature sounds good until nature gets a little too natural. Mostly we try to keep the outside out—dirt, rain, bugs and beasts, cold and hot, darkness.

Flying into Saint Louis the other day, truly a hot zone of the heartland, I thought about our struggle to beat the heat. From the airplane, a few minutes before landing I could see a familiar tableau: houses on blocks, on cul-de-sacs, on golf courses and rivers, many with shimmering blue circles and rectangles in the backyard; their own private kidney-shaped lakes, relief in sweltering Saint Louis, just a few feet from each house. The water in some of those pools is heated. Submerged, we want to be cool, but not cold. A friend of mine sets his pool water temperature 85 degrees. On a hot July 4, we loll in the water, sipping icy drinks.

A fortunate few in the ancient world got the idea that sweltering was not a given in the human condition. Wealthy Romans circulated cool water from the aqueducts through the walls of their homes. Roman emperor Elagabalus had snow brought to Rome via donkey trains. In second-century China, an enterprising inventor designed a system of rotary fans ten feet in diameter, manually operated. So back then, at least a few people were able to chill. But by and large, until just recently, human life was nasty, brutish, short, and, in many places on the globe, totally f-ing hot.

Some eighteen hundred years later, genius and available technology coalesced when a guy named Carrier devised a mechanism in which air was blown over water-cooled coils. Over time, in some parts of the world, chilling became general. In the United

States, AC is almost everywhere. In 85 percent of homes across the United States, there is shelter from the heat, brought to us by air conditioning.

I remember the shock and delight of encountering AC as a kid, real AC, not a fan, not window unit AC, I mean the glacial interiors of movie theaters, stores, and restaurants. Outside it was a muggy 90 degrees, inside a cool and dry 70.

The morning of the third day, a Saturday, I wake up on the couch, stiff, sticky, and cross.

My wife comes downstairs and sits beside me on the couch. She looks wilted but determined. "Shouldn't you gas up the generator?"

Shouldn't I just kill myself? I think.

When the power is out, day and night, all across the neighborhood, you hear the roar of generator engines powering refrigerators, sump pumps, and a few paltry light bulbs. To hot and humid we add this constant unnerving auditory hell.

"I guess so," I say. Then, "Hotel?"

She shakes her head no.

I tip over sideways on the couch. "Don't tell me you slept okay."

She stands up. "I'm going to go take a shower."

Right. We have plenty of hot water.

This is the history of the future: We melted ourselves. There will be no winning the war against hot. The machines we use to cool ourselves emit chemicals that intensify the greenhouse effect. The Maldives are two inches above sea level. It's getting hotter.

But we're not going down without a fight.

A few years ago my wife and I took some Italians to Manhattan. It was August. Our mission that weekend was boutique hopping. One of the visiting women owns a few boutiques in a town on the Adriatic. What's fashion look like in New York?

About the same way it looks in Italy.

But it feels different in New York. Fashion feels cold in New York, held at a chilly 68 degrees by NYC AC that is nothing short of miraculous. Two consecutive days, morning and afternoon, in the garment district, the meat-packing district, in and around the Villages, we shuffled up and down the sidewalks, in and out of shops. Midafternoon the temperature difference between inside and outside was approaching thirty degrees. To be inviting, or perhaps to provide a split second of relief to people in the streets, or maybe just out of raw stupidity, in many of these shops the doors were left open. Every forty feet or so, you passed through a wall, three feet thick, of cold air.

Crossing the threshold of one of these iceboxes to look at shoes, the Italians shuddered, put on jackets and sweaters, and wrapped pashminas around their necks, while my wife and I sighed with relief. So much cold! they complained. You Americans are crazy.

That night, up around Sixty-Sixth Street, we ate in a restaurant that was so cold, jackets and pashminas were not sufficient.

"Hot outside," the waiter said.

Tell him we're freezing, someone said in Italian.

"To drink?" the waiter asked. "Cold beer, chilled wine, iced tea?" He held up a stainless steel water pitcher, agitating its abundant ice, whetting, he must have imagined, our appetite for cold.

The third night, my wife takes the couch, while I descend to the basement. It's so hot in the house, dank feels good. Around 2:00 a.m. I am awakened by rolling thunder in the next room, where the furnace is. It's the launch of our AC, the furnace fan kicking on. We've got power.

I sit up, blinking. Lights. A house resuscitated. After a few minutes, I hear the basement door swing open.

"Hey," my wife says. "Are you coming back up?"

"Be right there," I say, picturing lights coming on around the neighborhood, generators shutting down, and AC units going back to work, helping us get back to normal.

"I can already feel the cool," she says.

I'm groggy and grateful for the coming chill and wonder how long it can last.

27 / Monsters

She's been reading in bed, beside me. When I wake up, my wife turns toward me and whispers, "We're so screwed."

Good morning.

It's probably politics she's reading about. Possibly the environment. I pull myself out of bed, tell her okay, but let's have coffee first.

Does it come with age, this habit of greeting the new day with prognostications of disintegration and doom? I remember a comic on *The Ed Sullivan Show* who made a joke about his wife's obsession with obituaries. They lived in New York City. Every morning she read obits in the newspaper, opened the phone book, and crossed out the names of the departed. That was ordinary morbidity. As in: Of course, we're *all* screwed, now let's see whose turn it was yesterday.

These days it seems like we're even more all screwed, and more than theoretically so. If you read the news, we are prematurely, peremptorily, collectively teetering-on-the-edge-of-extinction all screwed.

"Bugs," she says when she comes downstairs, iPad under her arm. "They say a great die-off is coming. Just think."

I've read about the bugs. "You shouldn't take that thing to bed with you," I say.

"I wake up."

"And read the news."

"Well?"

"It keeps you up."

I open the steam jet to froth milk for her cappuccino. She's saying something I cannot hear, powering up her iPad, shaking her head.

"It's a matter of sleep ecology," I tell her. "Experts say quit devices an hour before bed. And no devices in bed."

Bed is for sleep and for sex. That's it. I read that somewhere.

For a long time I worried about frogs, then the rain forests, then the coral reefs and bees. Even bats. But never bugs. I always figured that they would inherit the earth, that all the bug bombs and insecticide would only make them mutate into stronger, more resilient creatures. When the canaries in the coal mines went silent and it was curtains for us humans, the bugs, nature's Darwinian superpowers, would continue to buzz. They would prevail.

But I have to wonder. There does seem to be a dearth of bugs of late. When I was a kid, every summer we spent a few weeks in northern Michigan, on the shore of Lake Missaukee. Just the name hearkens to a time of innocence and balance between man and nature. On the drive up there, which took ninety minutes, you heard the continuous tick, smack, and splat of insects against the windshield. Forty-five minutes up the road, by the time we got to Harrison, if it started to rain and my father turned on wipers, a yellow buggy smear of legs and wings, of eyes and innards could make it impossible to see. On more than a few occasions, he had to pull off on the shoulder and scrub the mess so he could see the road.

A few years later, when I pumped gas at his service station, all summer I washed windshields plastered with splattered bug remains. It was man against nature, and the bugs, even though they were dead, tiny bits of them under your fingernails, clogging your sponge, and clinging to your squeegee, seemed to be winning.

These days, well into the self-serve era, I pump my own gas and can usually pass on the windshield. Last summer I drove from Detroit to Chicago and back, in August. Six hundred miles.

Two tanks of gas. One, two, okay, three or four bug fatalities in evidence on the windshield. That's all.

What happened?

Here's something you don't want to read in bed: "Climate-driven declines in arthropod abundance restructure a rainforest food web," from the PNAS *Journal* (Proceedings of the National Academy of Sciences of the United States of America). Authors Bradford C. Lister and Andres Garcia report evidence of the insect die-off and "synchronous declines in the lizards, frogs, and birds that eat arthropods." Studies suggest that bug biomass in the Puerto Rico Luquillo rain forest is way down. Rain forest life, it appears, is beginning to die from the bottom up.

In addition to the effects of rising temperatures on bug health, habitat loss and pesticides are playing a role. According to *Phys/Org*, a publication of Technical University Munich, "Over time and with the further deterioration of habitats as well as the collapse of entire habitat networks, the threat to widespread, 'undemanding' species also increases." By "undemanding" I assume they mean not exotic creatures of the rain forest but the more quotidian species, bugs that are your friends and neighbors: flies, mosquitoes, earwigs, ants. They too could be threatened.

In my lifetime, we haven't exactly tried to work with them. In our homes and backyards we threaten insects on a regular basis with sprays and powders, repellents and poisons with decidedly unfriendly names like Raid, Bite Back, Combat, Hunters Edge, Rambo, Mad Fight, Hell Gate, Tornado, Vortex, Master Attack, and (my personal favorite) Repellitor.

Then there are the industrial-strength killers—195 of them listed in the New England Vegetable Management Guide—some with names that overtly declare war on nature: Ambush, Assail, Besiege, Brigade, Capture, Defcon, Hatchet. Other names suggest agrochemical companies may have consulted their public relations departments: Advise, Entrust, Esteem, Fulfill, Respect, Seduce.

How will we protect bugs from ourselves? If life on the planet is dying from the bottom up, wouldn't we also be protecting ourselves from ourselves?

In the news today, residents of Toledo, Ohio, are engaged in a movement that would grant legal rights to Lake Erie. If a corporation can be regarded as a legal entity, why not a lake? The problem is algae blooms. (Blooms, a floral term with pleasant connotations, seems like an unfortunate word choice. Algae *bombs* might be better.) For years now, the lake, which provides drinking water for eleven million people and is integral to the economy of four states, has been plagued by rapid growth of algae, stimulated by fertilizer runoff.

Science News describes the calamity: "As more algae and plants grow, others die. This dead organic matter becomes food for bacteria that decompose it. With more food available, the bacteria increase in number and use up the dissolved oxygen in the water. When the dissolved oxygen content decreases, many fish and aquatic insects cannot survive. This results in a dead area."

Dead water with dead stuff in it, no surprise, is deadly to drink.

Existing laws do not adequately protect nature. Maybe it would help to give nature rights. There are precedents. In 2006 Tamaqua Borough, Pennsylvania, residents approved a rights-of-nature ordinance to curtail dumping of chemicals and sewage in open-pit mines. In nearby Pittsburgh, a rights-of-nature law limits fracking. Minnesota Ojibwes would like to extend rights to wild rice, "the right to pure water," in particular. In 1972, in *Sierra Club v. Morton*, the issue of nature having rights went to the Supreme Court. The court said no. But in his dissenting opinion, Justice William O. Douglas wrote that concerns about "ecological equilibrium" could lead to "the conferral of standing upon environmental objects to sue for their own preservation."

Should bugs have rights? Should we issue them green cards for our own good? What if they sue us?

Bug die-off science, some scientists argue, is inconclusive. It's apocalypse not. Or apocalypse maybe. How reliable is the data? How representative? Worldwide, around a million bug species have been identified; it's likely there are millions more. Studies of bug populations that have been done focused on limited geographical areas. Writing for the *Atlantic Monthly*, Ed Yong reports, "This spotty geographical spread makes it hard to know if insects are disappearing from some areas but recovering or surging in others."

I know what I know: I don't see dead bugs on my windshield. But does that mean there's a die-off? I know what I know: The weather in my town will be unseasonably cold next week, way below zero, and it's been snowing. Does that mean global warming in a hoax?

What's a flyswatter to do? How to think about bugs and us and our shared future?

Recently scientists found a female Wallace's giant bee (as long as an adult thumb) inside a tree in the Philippines, thought to be extinct for thirty-eight years. Maybe giant bees will make a comeback. Giant bugs, too.

Whose side are we on? Is it too late to form an alliance?

28 / Fit But

No, I will not start wearing one of those personal data devices anytime soon. To count my steps and hours of sleep, to monitor my blood pressure, to issue edifying, or depressing, reports on calories.

What if they figure out how to datify cheese consumption?

Around this time of year, I turn increasingly to cheese, for sustenance, comfort, and pleasure. Yes, the fat worries me. You can't spread triple cream brie on crostini and not pause, if only for a second, to think about your arteries. But, the wonders.

Those balls of di Stefano burrata that grace the cheese counter, made with milk whose fat content weighs in at 3.6 to 3.8 percent (conventional whole milk is 3.25), are nothing if not soft blobs of joy. *Bon Appétit* refers to burrata as "a purse of mozzarella filled with stracciatella [shreds of mozzarella in cream]." Let me be a shameless purse-snatcher.

And lately we have been buying a pecorino laced with black truffle, a cheese made from ewe's milk that, the producers say, calls to mind the "voluptuous pastures" of Lazio and Umbria.

One year, my wife and I stopped in Deruta, in central Umbria. It's a famous ceramics town. Spilling from every storefront were stacks of bowls, dishes, platters, pitchers, vases, and boxes, all beautiful stuff. Then, even better, there was lunch in Deruta, where we were served the local pecorino fresco on one of those ceramic platters. Our server invited us to drizzle truffle honey over the cheese. We did, and it was a conversion experience

There is already plenty of impersonal cheese data out there. Eighty percent of cheese production worldwide is made from cow's milk, 13 percent from buffalo's, 5 percent from sheep's, goat's, and camel's milk. The French eat more cheese than any other European, annually around 26 kilos per capita, way more than an American eats (15.4 kilos). A typical supermarket in France stocks as many as 130 different types of cheese, a cheese shop, up to 100 cheeses. The French eat cheese, and they are thin. Cheese is part of the French paradox, their fat, sugar, alcohol, bread, butter, cheese, pastry, caffeine, and nicotine regimen that keeps them thin.

Also they walk.

I walk. I even sort of run. When I do, I walk and run for cheese.

Back in the eighties I decided I was going to be a runner. I read the Jim Fixx book on running and bought a pair of snazzy shorts. At parties, talking to runners, I learned about their improved sleep and their shin splints, their dietary preferences and their bowel movements. This was, of course, in the pre-data era. There was no Fitbit, no Jawbone, no Runtastic or Vivoactive or Misfit Shine. You looked at your wristwatch, you counted laps or miles, you went home and stood on the bathroom scales. You reflected on the outcome: you felt good, you felt bad. You ran through pain. You sought the runner's high. In conversations, most runners eventually made the same claim: running was good for your head.

Back then I wanted to improve everything, so why not my head? I bought a primitive musical device called a Walkman so I could listen to music while I ran. I made a few cassette tapes and headed for the track.

For starters I went out on Tuesday and Thursday afternoons. The idea was to take it slow, ease into it. I saw the same co-worker out there every day, a social science guy much older than me. He had stubby legs like mine, also a sitter's body like mine. He ran two to three miles to my two to three laps. When he lapped me, which he inevitably did, repeatedly, he yelled over his shoulder at me.

Nice day today, Sonny.

Looking good, Sonny.

Pick up the pace, Sonny

One day I arrived as he was leaving. He cleaned his glasses on his sweaty T-shirt and said hello. His face was red, his breathing even. (The heart rate and breathing of a seasoned runner, Jim Fixx said sometime before he died running, have a very short recovery period.)

"Do you like wearing that thing?" He pointed at the headset I had wrapped around my neck. No one had thought of earbuds yet. This was a springy thing that clamped speakers to my ears. It slid around on my head and required constant adjustment as I ran.

"I like the music," I said.

He slid his glasses back on. "What are we listening to today?"

"Today," I said, "it's Gregorian chant." This was part of my running-as-a-pathway-to-equanimity regimen.

"Latin."

"Yes."

"A cappella."

"Yes."

The chanters sang, *Vidi aquam egredientem de templo, a latere dextro, alleluia. Et omnes, ad quos pervenit aqua ista, salvi facti sunt.* "I saw water coming forth from the temple on the right side, alleluia. And all those to whom this water came were saved."

He smiled at me and shook his head. "Does it help?"

It didn't help. In fact, I would admit now, it was kind of distracting.

He said, "I like the idea of a bunch of monks jogging."

"Alleluia," I said. And pressed play.

Today we have data, tons of it. It's supposed to help. You strap on one of those thingies and collect data without even knowing it, all day long, every step you take. Our goal, experts say, should be ten thousand steps. According to Catrine Tudor-Locke, director of the Walking Behavior Laboratory at Pennington Biomedical Research Center in Baton Rouge, Louisiana, the average American adult takes around fifty-nine hundred steps a day. We need to get busy. Later we can upload our data and assess our progress.

If you work at it, you can quantify much of your life, reducing it to data sets. You can achieve the data-driven life. But do we want to? The Wordsworth poem, "The Tables Turned," comes to mind; these lines, in particular, near the end of the poem:

> Sweet is the lore which Nature brings;
> Our meddling intellect
> Mis-shapes the beauteous forms of things:—
> We murder to dissect.

Supposedly on his office door, Einstein hung a sign that read "Not everything that counts can be counted, and not everything that can be counted counts." An important caution in a data-dizzy world.

A school where I taught reduced the reading process to thirty-seven distinct measurable skills. Kids put in a lot of workbook time. They took a lot of tests. Reading improvement remained flat. Today assessment takes up a lot of time in public school. You assess so you can improve teaching. What do you measure? What do you do with the data? How much murder is required for how much improvement?

One day my brother and I were talking about how quickly the summer months pass, in contrast to when we were kids. "You know why that is?" he said. "When you're a kid, the summer months are a pretty large fraction of the life you've lived. Every year older you get, the smaller that fraction becomes."

My brother is a numbers guy. I used to be, until I took a left turn into letters.

I was working on some science curriculum with a physicist around this time. The physicist developed lab experiments using various data-acquisition devices; I did the experiments and wrote about them. After talking to my brother that day I decided to do what my physicist pal would do: work up the numbers, use the Excel chart wizard, and make a pretty picture. The results were not pretty. In fact, they were just plain depressing. When you're one year old, three summer months are 25 percent of your lifetime. At five years of age, they're 5 percent; at age twenty-five, 1 percent. From there it's all downhill, except there's hardly any hill left. You skid along, getting closer and closer to zero. And then you die.

Sometimes you just don't want to see the data. You don't want to know the number. When my blood pressure was running high, I bought a battery-operated cuff I could use at home. I found if I took my blood pressure five or six times, I could eventually get to an acceptable number.

I want to be fit, but I also want to enjoy cheese. No Fitbit for me. I walk, I run, I listen to Bach, Brubeck, and the Beatles, sometimes the Spice Girls. I look at my wristwatch, count laps and miles, weigh myself on the bathroom scale. That's enough data.

29 / Quit It

"Table for five," I say to the greeter. "I think there's a reservation."

She looks for the name I give her, then glances up at me. "Is the rest of your party here?"

"Almost," I hear myself say, when, really, it's anyone's guess. It's an end-of-semester lunch with colleagues. They're giving and grading exams, having last-minute conferences with students. Not me. I'm retired.

She looks around. The restaurant, a popular joint in Detroit, is mostly empty at the moment. Within the next half hour, it will be packed.

When she turns back to me, I tell her they're on their way.

She leads me to a table near the front of the restaurant. Once I'm seated, to pass time and avoid further eye contact with the greeter, I take out my phone. Next to me, two thirty-somethings are also busy with their phones, dispensing with eye contact. Surveying the room, at every occupied table I notice how many individuals, in groups and by themselves, are dining quietly by phone light.

Which gives me pause. Can I do it?

Can I put my phone away, just sit, and be fully present?

According to a recent article in the *New York Times*, it might not be a bad idea to put down your cell phone. "An increasing body of evidence," Catherine Price writes, "suggests that the time we spend on our smartphones is interfering with our sleep, self-esteem, relationships, memory, attention spans, creativity, productivity and problem-solving and decision-making skills." All that and so much more, I'm sure.

Try letting your mind wander for a change, another *Times* article says.

For God's sake, why can't we just BE, the way we used to be?

In the restaurant today, I decide to be decisive. I put my phone away. I'll try being. I'll open myself to the environment, to the mini-scenes taking place around me, let my mind wander.

I survey the wall of liquor bottles behind the bar, which reminds me of the first bar I frequented, at eighteen years of age, a moldy Rathskeller rank with the scent of old mold and spilled beer; glance out the window at the homeless man across the street singing his heart out, the same guy I saw last time I was here; remember my old friend Ludlow, who lived in a cramped apartment just around the corner from the restaurant, an apartment so small he kept his artificial Christmas tree up—and lit—year around; try to listen to conversation going on around me, one of my favorite indoor sports, more difficult these days because 1) people in restaurants are frequently too busy attending to their phones to engage in entertaining conversation, and 2) in my dotage I have grown somewhat hard of hearing, which makes me wonder: Is anyone in this room wearing a hearing aid? I look around, checking out ears.

Motion outside the restaurant catches my attention, a solitary guy smoking on the sidewalk.

And here comes the floating waiter, the tall one with the light step who does not move his arms or shoulders while in stride; the look on his face is beatific. He combines being and workingness.

After ten minutes of just being (including moments of self-consciousness—*Why is that guy just sitting there? Doesn't he have anything to do?*), I see my colleagues push through the restaurant entrance. At the table we catch up: How are we? We are good. The wait? No, not long, thanks, just ten minutes or so. Retirement suits me just fine. Yes, I miss the work, especially the students, but no, not the grading and no, you're right, not those students. We consult the menu and the wine list, recite orders to the beatific waiter, who nods a slow, knowing nod and, flexing his memory, writes nothing down.

A few minutes later, he returns with wine, sets down glasses. I hold up a hand. No wine for me, thanks. My colleagues look shocked. What?

Call it a pause or hiatus, I say. A reset.

I've arrived at the quit. Another one.

I'm reminded of a few lines from Sylvia Plath: "Dying / Is an art, like everything else. / I do it exceptionally well."

So it is with quitting. An art. But unlike Plath and her dying, like everyone else, I'm not very good at it.

I smoked cigarettes for a couple years out of high school, until I tapered off, substituting joints for cigarettes. The quit lasted a few years. Then, through graduate school and into the early years of my work and married life, long after I had given up the joints, I smoked cigarettes on weekends, at wedding receptions and cocktail parties, then heavily through the writing of a doctoral dissertation.

This was before the patch, before nicotine gum, before the robust acknowledgment that, medically speaking, smoking was a bummer.

Ludlow was in a constant state of quitting. On and off he employed a set of special filter attachments that reduced tar and nicotine. Ten filters, ten weeks, a gradual reduction in carcinogens helped you wean yourself from the habit. In some cases. He used them for a few years, to regulate how much of a hit he needed. Today I'm a five, he would say. Another day he was a seven. At a Christmas party one night in his tiny apartment, I noticed he was off the filter cessation program altogether. I'm going full Marlboro, he said with a shrug. For the holidays, you know, you just need a good boost of nicotine. Next week he was back on the filters.

I finally quit cold turkey. It was difficult. And liberating.

In a casual survey of the literature on quitting, I find lots of how-to articles. How to quit smoking, vaping, drinking; how to quit sugar, Facebook, weed; how to quit your job; how to quit saying yes, quit saying no, quit worrying about people's expectations, quit holding onto the past, quit making to-do lists. You'll find the five, the ten, the fifteen, the twenty-one things you need to quit in order to be happy. How to quit being bored.

If I looked a little longer, I'm sure there would be a five-step program on how to quit quitting.

Among all the subjects in quit lit, the smartphone is conspicuously absent. Jeremiads, yes; screen time is making us dumb, antisocial, forgetful, etc.; invitations to quit, no.

When I was still in the classroom, many of my students couldn't go five minutes without picking up their phones. A recent study of two thousand Americans found the average person looks at their phone eighty times a day; 10 percent of the study participants, three hundred times a day. At the height of my smoking addiction, I smoked a pack a day. Twenty cigarettes, at six minutes a cigarette, is two hours a day. You can find out how much time you spend on your phone. Me? About the same as smoking, a couple hours a day. That does not make me happy. How much of that time do I actually use my phone *as a phone*? Very little.

"Bow wow."

When I was eighteen and had come out as a smoker, one of father's pals summed up the habit with those two words. "Every ten minutes, every thirty minutes," he said, "bow wow." He mimed reaching in his pocket and pulling out a cigarette.

For some time now I've been aware of the phantom buzz. Around the part of my body where I keep my phone, often in a jacket pocket, the same place I kept a pack of cigarettes, I feel a buzz. I don't hear it; but I definitely feel it. *Was that my phone? Is that a text? An email?* Even when my phone isn't there, I feel the buzz. It freaks me out.

Phone addiction used to be generational. Those darn kids. Adults are catching up, big time. A recent study by Common Sense Media, conducted online and by phone, surveyed five hundred pairs of parents and teenagers, and found that "while parents feel increasingly glued to their phones, attitudes among teenagers moved in the opposite direction." Young people are still more phone addicted than older people, but the difference is narrowing. Kids are saying to their parents, Put it away.

More adults are taking their devices to bed with them, using them within five minutes of going to sleep, waking up to check them, looking at them within five minutes of getting up in the morning. With the concomitant degradation of sleep.

And the degradation of shared space.

Who doesn't have an older friend or relative who, new to the smart device, hauls it out to share photos or video (*Hey, look at this!*) or disappears into the digital cocoon while the visit, party, and/or dinner conversation goes on around them?

Put it away.

The addiction is powerful. "Dopamine starts you seeking," according to *Psychology Today*, "then you get rewarded for the seeking which makes you seek more. It becomes harder and harder to stop looking at email, stop texting, or stop checking your cell phone to see if you have a message or a new text."

Smartphone is the new cigarette. Dopamine is the new nicotine.

When I quit smoking, I went through a period of time when I didn't know what to do with my hands. In muscle memory, I could feel the repetitive motion of raising a hand to my mouth. It was eerie, and unnerving. The smartphone now presents a similar repetitive motion problem. Take out your device and check in. Check in for what? Nothing in particular. It's just something to do with your hands.

The reviews are in for a new device, the NoPhone, which is the equivalent of methadone therapy for device addiction. Says *Fast Company*: "A security blanket phone addicts are taking seriously." *Time* magazine: "A simulation of your comfort object, helping you slowly abandon it." The *New York Times*: "Always have a rectangle of plastic to clutch."

That's what it is: a rectangle of black plastic with the dimensions and weight of a digital device, on sale today at Amazon for twelve dollars. You can't make calls, you can't check texts, email, or the internet; you can't consult your calendar or find out how close you are to taking ten thousand steps. You can't play solitaire. The manufacturer describes it thus: "With a thin, light and completely wireless design, the NoPhone acts as a surrogate to any smart mobile device, enabling you to always have a rectangle of smooth, cold plastic to clutch without forgoing any potential engagement with your direct environment. Never again experience the unsettling feeling of flesh on flesh when closing your hand."

Slip it in the hip pocket of your jeans, in a shirt or jacket pocket, close to your heart. Just knowing it's there will give you a sense of security.

That day in the restaurant, five of us got through most of a lunch without anyone taking out his phone. They had wine. I had a gin and tonic without the gin.

There is real pleasure in quitting. For me, it's the forgetting and remembering. You forget about wanting a cigarette, about wanting alcohol. When you remember, it's a rush. *I don't need that anymore. I forgot all about it. I have control.*

Less phone time? Today I'm not sure I can do it, not sure I want to do it. That day is coming. I can feel it—in the phantom buzz.

30 / A Suite, a Swim, a Fish

Nobody told me there would be a Gulf of Mexico.

It was October 2005. What little I knew about Galveston, Texas, I owed entirely to Glen Campbell. His song of that title, written by Jimmy Webb, was released in February 1969. I was sixteen. I had a girlfriend. The song played on the AM radio in my red vw bug when we bombed around town or drove down to the drive-in theater in Saginaw. Good song, crappy radio. I never bothered to listen carefully to the lyrics. I hummed along indiscriminately and waited for the sad and yearning turn in GC's voice when he sang, "Galveston, oh Galveston, I am so afraid of dying," missing the references to the sea that came earlier in the song, to the sea winds, to the sea waves, to the beautiful woman standing by the water.

So when the cab pulled up to the hotel that day in Galveston, and I found myself at the edge of a wide beach, looking out to sea, I thought, *No one told me there would be a Gulf of Mexico*. I was not prepared.

My colleague and I were in town for an English teacher conference. We checked into the hotel where registration and the meetings and luncheons would be held, right across the street from the Gulf. Good location. Crappy rooms. We were on the ground floor. There were bars on the windows and the doors. My room smelled of old mold and a chemical floral deodorizer-disinfectant. Under foot, I was sure the scuzzy carpet would feel damp if I took off my shoes. I didn't.

Five hotels up the road was a Hilton. My colleague and I had just published a textbook together and were working on a second book, hoping for years of royalty checks. The week before, we had gone to a conference in Santa Monica, next to another fabled body of water, where we had experienced Hilton comfort.

I called her and told her, Don't unpack. Meet me up front.

When we met back in the lobby I said, "Let's go."

"It's not that bad," she said.

"Yes, it is that bad," I said. And it seemed clear, the longer we were there, the badder it would get.

We walked up the road. Yes, there were rooms available at the Hilton, also on the ground floor. Yes, they were more money. I thought about those bars, about the bad smell. We made the move.

That was the first of three good decisions I made that weekend.

I was raised with an it's-not-that-bad ethos. I learned not to make a fuss, not to draw attention, not to be demanding. Maybe it was Midwest. Or maybe Methodist. Or just my parents' dubious gift to me. On your birthday, presented with actual gift that you didn't really like that much, you smiled, nodded your head, and said you liked it. It wasn't that bad.

In time I learned there was another point of view.

A year or so after we were married, I remember my wife's reaction to a gift my mother gave her. It was our first Christmas. She opened the package and frowned. She looked at my mother and said, "Do you still have the sales slip?"

On my mother's face, a quizzical look. I felt an uncomfortable blip in my blood pressure.

"Can I take this back?" my wife said.

Aghast, I asked her later, "How could you do that?"

She shrugged and gave me a quizzical look. "Why would I keep something I don't like?" she said. "Isn't that a waste? Wouldn't that make your mother unhappy?"

"Yes, but . . ."

But she had made a fuss. But she had made the gift giver feel bad.

Down in Galveston, at the Bars-on-the-Windows Regency, I said we had decided to make a change and could we cancel? And they said yes. I didn't want to make them feel bad. Neither did I want to take my shoes off in that terrible room.

The next day, in full sun on a glorious afternoon, I was body-surfing waves in the Gulf of Mexico, looking up at my hotel room. That's right, up. The ground floor rooms we checked into the day before had noisy AC wall units that ran continuously, barely keeping the rooms cool. The sound was deafening. And somehow, I had the idea that Legionnaires' disease and air conditioning units were correlated. I didn't open my carry-on. Could I do it, twice in one day?

At the front desk I asked if there might not be another room. I didn't want to appear difficult and demanding, but why should I be unhappy?

"Last week," I explained, "I stayed in the Santa Monica Hilton, one of the nicest hotels I've ever been in." This one, I added in the most apologetic way I could, was kind of a disappointment.

Evan smiled at me over his glasses. He said he understood. "Let's take a look, Mr. Bailey," he said.

He moved me to the twelfth floor, a suite with a Gulf view. The AC was silent and sufficient. I don't know what the bedsheets' thread count was. Approaching four digits, I think. Heavenly pillows. What comfort. There was no additional charge.

"You did what?" my colleague said later.

"You just have to ask," I said.

That was the second good decision I made that weekend.

My default position in most situations is still "it's not that bad." A few weeks ago my wife and I were out to dinner with a couple friends. A crowded place. Reservations made a few weeks in advance. We went through the menu, noticing, as we did so, a man sitting at a table outside on the veranda. He was with three women. His shirt was unbuttoned to his waist. Ample belly. Lots of belly and chest hair. Lots of gold.

When our server returned with drinks I asked about the mackerel. On the menu the fish was described as brined, not cooked, with a cucumber relish.

"It's in season right now," the server said. "Light, like ceviche."

I asked: "Served cold?"

"Warm," he said. He took orders around the table, heritage tomato salad, carpaccio, eggplant parmigiana, scallops. When he came back to me, I was still dithering. He said he really liked the mackerel. He was recommending it to everyone.

When our food came, we gestured in the direction of veranda guy with the exposed hairy belly. The server nodded and smiled, said he had noticed him too.

"Would you?" one of our friends said, holding out his phone to the server. "Take a group photo?"

The server took a few shots of us. In one of them he positioned himself so that the exhibitionist outdoors was in full view. It was a good joke.

The mackerel was nothing like ceviche. It was an inch and a half thick slab, with a layer of skin on the bottom side of the chunk. Tough as a piece of overdone steak. I poked it, I sawed at it. With a little effort, I found I could tear at it and shred it. But the problem remained.

"So?" my wife said.

"Can you make leather from fish?"

"If you don't like it, you should send it back. The chef would want to know."

"It's not that bad." I swear I said it. I didn't send it back.

After a night in the Hilton and a morning of conference meetings down at that other place, my colleague and I had a forgettable conference lunch. Outside it was sunny and warm. Up in Michigan, I told everyone I saw, the colors were changing. People were going to the cider mill, which seemed charming. It *was* charming. But I was in Galveston. Outside was the sun, the Gulf.

And I had come unprepared. No swimsuit.

The third decision.

Midafternoon, after the conference coffee break, I decided to skip the next session. I walked back to the Hilton, went upstairs, and changed into a pair of jeans and T-shirt. Outside I walked across the street to the beach. Lake Michigan size waves were rolling in. I pulled off my shirt and stripped to my skivvies, feeling slightly exhibitionist. I just couldn't worry about other people. I waded in for a swim.

That night, when I called my wife and she asked how things were going, I told her, in that weird lingo we use without thinking, that it wasn't too bad. "Not too bad" is a small step up from "not that bad" and significantly better than just plain bad.

Not too bad? In point of fact, it was actually damn good.

31 / Me and Velociraptor and Forrest Gump

We've just finished our tour of the lower Antelope Slot Canyon tour, outside Page, Arizona. Along the way our guide, Ryan, has been giving us a short course in geological history, which my wife translates from English into Italian for our friends Luigi and Adele. Her translations are brilliant, embellished by her impressive knowledge of American Indian culture.

In our little group of twelve people is a woman our age, dressed in fashionable khaki hiking-touring attire. She's by herself, shooting pictures with a very big camera. I'm thinking, journalist? Along the way, it begins to seem like she's edging closer to us, lurking. I'm trying to gauge her expression. Is she peeved by these translations? Does she think they're slowing us down?

But then, could we go any slower? I estimate, between the twelve of us, we're traveling at five hundred photos a minute. At the bottom of a ladder we will have to climb, I turn to this woman and say, "I'm taking all these pictures. They'll probably all look the same when I get home."

She holds up her camera and smiles. "I'm Italian," she says, in very accented English.

Now I get it. She's been listening.

From this point on, she stays close to us. Ryan points out rock formations—the eagle, the lady of the wind, a lizard, a bear. They even have an Abraham Lincoln.

When we get outside, she and my wife, and Luigi and Adele break off from the group to have a chat, while Ryan concludes the tour by pointing to dinosaur tracks in the rock.

"Hey, guys," I say to them, "dinosaur tracks." Looks like velociraptor. (I know my *Jurassic Park*.)

The footprint is six inches long. It says, millions of years later, "Hey, I was here."

The next morning in the breakfast room, between bites of automated pancake and scrambled eggs, I read T-shirts people are wearing. Thin woman with a limp, "London." Tall late-middle-aged man, "Cottonwood 300, Two Wheels, Three Days, 5280 vert." Male senior with a bushy mustache, "Durango and Silverton." Muscular man in his forties, "Texas." His muscular wife, "Good Stuff."

The room fills up. "Alaska." "San Francisco." "New York." A thin young guy in work boots and pants walks past me; he must be a construction worker. "Zero Travel," it says on his bright yellow shirt. He's up early, going to work today. He'll get somewhere eventually.

On the wall at the far end of the breakfast room is a large world map, with the United States on the far left. A couple Asian kids are looking at it, one of them on the left, pointing to the exact spot on earth where she is standing at this exact moment, the other in front, with a camera, taking her picture.

Hey, we were here.

Next day, on our drive across Monument Valley, we're helping Luigi and Adele with their English. We're concentrating on hiking and food English on this trip, *un viaggio linguistico*, Luigi calls it. This day is trail English, mostly one-syllable Anglo-Saxon words. Path. Sand, rock, dirt. Front, back. Snake, deer. We also repeat a couple useful two-syllable words—ladder, backpack, chipmunk—and, anticipating dinner, practice saying a common three-syllable word, hamburger. They say ahm-BOUR-gare.

Around 10:00 a.m. we get out of the car at a place called Bucktank Draw, our first hike of the day.

Creek, brook. Cave, bridge. Wash.

Later, crossing the Valley of the Gods, we pull off the road a few times to take a picture. On our third stop, I see it. I mean the big it, in the Jack Kerouac *On the Road* sense of the term. IT.

I've been looking for the iconic Utah shot, the long two-lane highway gently sloping downhill, stretching out to the horizon, desert wastelands on all sides, a couple lonely buttes in the distance. The great vast, empty America, a place where hope springs eternal, with great difficulty in some places.

On this stop we are not alone.

We're on Highway 163, just south of Mexican Hat, twenty or thirty of us standing by the side of the road, waiting for traffic to clear. By traffic I mean a lone vehicle crawling up the long hill.

People are parked on the shoulder, standing next to their cars, waiting for an opportunity to claim the middle of the road, all alone, so they can take the picture. What good is a photo of this road if there's a car coming up the road or, for that matter, a couple guys with goofy hats in the picture?

Squatting in the sand, a guy with a lot of tattoos is powering up a drone. He's going to rise above the rest of us.

"Me and my buddy," he says, "we got a whole car full of camera gear."

I hold up my iPhone.

"Everyone wants the Forrest Gump shot."

I tell him I've never seen the movie.

"Me neither," he says. "But this piece of road is in that movie. Kinda made it famous."

A woman walks up behind us, watching. On her shirt it says "I love my church." She says we should also drive over to Dead Horse Point to get a shot of the Thelma and Louise cliff.

Cliff, I think. Saving that word for Luigi and Adele.

The woman waits. A big truck blows past us. "The end of the movie?" she says. "You know?"

Yes, I've seen that one.

It takes fifteen minutes for me to finally get my shot. I'm not sure what I'm going to do with the picture, but I feel good, fulfilled in a weird way.

In 1971, on my first road trip, I drove out to Colorado with some pals and tried to be a working hippie in Breckenridge for the summer. I had a Kodak Instamatic. In four weeks I shot three rolls of film, rolls of twenty-four. Most of the shots were mountains. When I got home, and developed and looked at the pictures, not only did they not begin to do justice to what I had seen, I didn't even know where I was when I took the photos.

They just said, Hey, I was somewhere. Which was sort of okay. But also not.

I don't know what became of those photos.

A few years later I drove through Yosemite with some friends. At the visitors' center I bought a light-blue T-shirt with "Go Climb a Rock" written on the front in bold black letters. I loved that shirt. I felt validated. It made me feel worldly. Hey, I was there.

A few years after that, my wife and I were in San Francisco with our kids. She took some pictures with her Nikon, mostly cityscapes. Among them is a photo of her with Tony Bennett, standing outside a restaurant called the Tazze D'Oro in North Beach. Tony looks just like Tony, smiling, spiffy. My wife looks just like herself, smiling and giddy. I think I know where that picture is. Somewhere in a very big box.

A friend of ours said once: always put a person in a picture. Hey, I was here. With him.

My wife does this. Go stand over there, she says. Later, in the picture, there I am, in front of a mountain, a valley, a church, small by association.

An acquaintance back home does sports news on TV. When I went to his house once, he took me down in the basement, which served as his photo gallery. On the wall were photos of him with sports celebrities. A photo of him with Muhammad Ali. A photo of him with Sparky Anderson. A photo of him with Magic Johnson. A photo of him with Jack Morris. Two walls, a hundred photos.

Him and a famous athlete. Hey, the photos say, I was with him. Great by association.

After Bucktank Draw, after the Forrest Gump photo, we drive from Moab to Arches. More one-syllable words. Fence, gate, path. Arch, bridge. Edge, cliff, slip.

In this car we are four people, three cameras, two languages. At the end of the first week, Luigi says he's taken fifteen hundred photos. That's one camera. I figure together we're heading for ten thousand images. We'll go home and look and look. Hey, I was there. And there. And there. In the middle of those infinite landscapes, great by association, small in comparison. We will look and look, then file the images away in their 0s and 1s, infinitely small bits.

Not out of nowhere exactly, I get an email from Elena one night. She's the Italian woman we met in Page. My wife gave her my email address. Elena says, Hi, maybe we can swap some photos, by email.

Hi, I say back, where are you now? I know she's somewhere out there. For the time being, we're all out there somewhere.

32 / Rock Me

I'm eating my second push-button pancake in the hotel breakfast room. On the television I can see something festive is happening. It's a bicycle race or a foot race, maybe a parade.

The pancake is not a precooked, warmed-up, ersatz mistake. Inside a machine the size of an old-fashioned breadbox is a plastic bag of premixed pancake batter. You push a button on the left, the box emits a quiet hum, and three minutes later a perfectly round, medium-rare comestible gradually rolls out of the side of the machine. Think pancake fax.

With push-button yogurt (plain low-fat Greek or vanilla fat-intact American), push-button juices, and push-button coffee, you can make a good start to the day.

Glancing up again at the TV, I realize it's Earth Day. I'm looking at how they celebrate Earth Day in Arizona.

Who doesn't remember their first Earth Day? On April 22, 1970, the first Earth Day ever, I was six weeks from high school graduation. It had been three years since the Summer of Love, a year since the Tet Offensive. Eight miles north of town, Dow Chemical, napalm producer and unfettered polluter of the Tittabawassee River, and Dow Corning, plastic wrap and breast implant manufacturer, were reminders that the earth belonged to us, too, and Earth Day had a purpose, an urgent one, even.

It was a bright sunny day, I remember that much. And a number of us walked out of school, though whether we had the blessing of Mr. Haenke, the school principal, I do not recall. I would like to think it was an act of civil disobedience.

This morning I'm grateful for the good hotel breakfast because our room last night was challenging.

For some reason we were checked into a handicapped room, which means oddly located light switches, a closet with hangers and rail at waist level, no visible electrical outlets (how that helps a handicapped person I do not know), and a wheelchair-friendly shower. (Our friends, for the same price, got the room with a fireplace, with a small sitting room, with frontage to the deck facing red rock buttes.)

"No water pressure," I hear my wife say from the shower. "And the thingy doesn't work."

Huh?

It's the handheld nozzle attached to a hose, an accessory she absolutely requires. I have a look. It's a bad situation. She's not taking a shower. She's taking a dribble.

I ought to be able to fix that. Three consecutive years I took people to a moderately crappy, extremely affordable hotel in Florence, ridiculously named Hotel Versailles. Everyone had a private bath but me. I didn't mind. I was by myself. But the bathroom I used, up five steps and down the hall from my room, had a showerhead that was almost totally stopped up. It squirted and fizzed.

The first year I stayed there, I found a hardware store and bought a showerhead. Problem solved. Every year I took the showerhead home with me and took it back with me on the next trip. The fourth year, Versailles went under.

In our handicapped shower, the problem eludes me.

I call the front desk, they offer to send a plumber. For one night? Who wants a plumber in their hotel bathroom, at night?

The mild irritation I feel at the altered space and accommodations in the room must be nothing compared to what handicapped people have felt their whole lives in spaces not made hospitable to them. This room indicates we've made progress, I don't know how much, but when I reach down into the closet for a hanger, I tell myself: get a grip.

And outside, at 7:00 a.m. in Sedona, is cloudless blue sky, red rock towers, arches, buttes, mesas, a place and a planet that still need Earth Day, need it every day.

33 / Faces in the Stone

I've been having doubts about my hat. It's a hiker's hat with a full brim all the way around, and a drawstring that hangs in front of my ears and that can be cinched under my chin. I bought it sort of on the fly. It was a careless oh-what-the-hell purchase. I knew I would need a hat. In three weeks' time we would be walking eight national parks.

Unlike my wife, who looks great in hats (and she will tell you so, and it is true), a hat on my head can look ridiculous. When I buy a hat, attention must be paid.

The problem is, this hat is blue. And it feels and looks permanent-press. A hat with soul has to have some wrinkles. It should look like it's taken some abuse. This hat is technologically improved, wrinkle-, water-, and soul-resistant.

One of my first impressions when we get on a trail is that everyone has a better hat than I do. After we hike a few trails in Canyonlands, I revise this impression. I see some really terrible hats. On a continuum, dorky hats on one end, cool hats on the other, mine definitely falls in the medium dork range. I think about remedies. One night, back at the hotel, I dunk my hat in a sink full of water and tie it up. Next morning, when I untie it, the hat pops back into its stay-press shape.

It's fatuous, I know, to be preoccupied with my hat in these places. To walk in these parks should be a spiritual experience. At the end of one day, at Arches, driving out of the park, I see a bearded man in red shorts and a T-shirt stand by the side of the road, looking. He is not taking a picture. He is just looking.

You see this in the parks—the long gaze. I guarantee you, he is not thinking about his hat.

Late one afternoon, leaving Dead Horse Point visitors' center, we're heading for the Green River lookout. My wife has decided to introduce Luigi and Adele to American Indian music. Luigi pulls a CD out of his pack. It's called *Sacred Spirit: Chants and Dances of the Native Americans*. We listen to "How the West Was Lost," "Winter Ceremony," "The Counterclockwise Circle Dance," "Celebrate Wild Rice," "Brandishing the Tomahawk," "Heal the Soul," and "Intertribal Song the Stop the Rain."

They're good songs, with plenty of soulful potential, mostly played in the key of E.

E for electric, that is. We hear drums, both real and synthetic; occasional voices, sampled chants of Navajo, Pueblo, and Sioux tribes; and a lot of synthesized music. The music is soulful and techno. Mostly techno, the work of Claus Zundel (a.k.a. "The Brave"), Ralf Hamm, and Markus Staab, of a recently discovered new-age tribe in Germany. After an hour or so, in the car we make an intertribal decision to stop the music.

That night I contemplate what to do. Run over my hat with the car. Dunk it in a mud puddle. Pile rocks on top of it. Punch its lights out. Standing in front of the bathroom mirror before bed, I put on the hat, tighten the chin string on top of the hat, pulling the side brims up, Aussie style. It's a small but appreciable move in the right direction on the hiker hat continuum.

A few days later we hike along Taylor Creek in Kolob Canyon, in the northwest section of Zion. The hike follows the creek for two and a half miles. Along the way you cross the creek dozens of times, stepping on rocks down the bank into the stream, rock-hopping across the water and up the other bank. I can't help but think of Japhy Ryder skipping down a mountainside in Kerouac's *The Dharma Bums*, a book that made me want to hike and climb when I was in college.

The focus and concentration on movement, boot feel, the sound of the stream and wind create a spiritual vibe that day, but the real spiritual whammy occurs when we get to the end of the trail.

At the end of the trail, the Double Arch Alcove is a great damp shady space that forms a huge natural amphitheater, one of those natural acoustical marvels. A group of Mormon girls are swishing about in their long dresses and sandals. Then they stop, form themselves into two rows, and begin to sing.

Zion is a busy place. The Taylor Creek trail is crowded this day, even in late April. Other hikers approaching the Alcove, hearing the singing, stop and lift their heads and fall silent. The sound is full and haunting and uplifting; it is pure heaven. The girls sing all four verses of "Our Mountain Home So Dear."

Then they stop. Everyone applauds. The girls go back to skipping along to the trail, and then they're gone. We who heard them remain, standing in hushed silence.

For a few days I contemplate different hats. I look at them in visitor centers and shops we walk into. I don't want a hat with Bryce written on it, or Capitol Reef, or Moab. I want a nondenominational hat.

In the Zion trolley, next to the map indicating the nine stops and trails to access from each stop, I see this quotation: "Wilderness is not a luxury but a necessity of the human spirit, and as vital to our lives as water and good bread" (Edward Abbey). We get off the trolley at the ninth stop, to hike the Narrows. You walk ankle deep and knee deep in the Virgin River, using a staff to help keep your footing. The bottom is stony, the current a steady pull.

Every so often, you remember to stop and look up—up at the sheer cliffs that rise straight and high over your head, some of them several hundred feet. You struggle to maintain balance at these vertiginous moments. It's wilderness. You're cold and unsteady, but still you get kind of drunk in the moment. You marvel at the millions of years it took to create these cliffs and canyons. Some people see God's hand at work, others the long grinding and sluicing and slow pressure and lift of tectonic plates.

When we get to the Colorado River a few days later, I begin to see faces in the stone. Same cliffs, made millions of years ago, same science. I think of these cliffs, back there in the infinite past, as time before God. The faces in the rock come at me—cubist human figures sculpted in stone, mostly men, none of them smiling, none wearing hats.

Lizard, pig, frog, turtle.

A palace.

"Do you see that one?" I ask my wife. I point to the top of the canyon, a cliff face half a mile down the river, tell her to follow the three stairs down, left to right, then look straight down.

"Where?"

"He looks biblical," I say.

"I see him," the woman next to me says. She lifts her camera to take a picture. A few other people on the raft see what I see; others don't look.

Around the next bend, I see Gonzo, the Muppet. Then some Egyptian-looking figures. Then some faces of indigenous peoples.

The cliffs contain multitudes. We see what we want to see up there, what's there and what's not there.

I pull off my hat and put it back on. It's not perfect, but I need it.

34 / Where We Are Was Once a Sea

When you get to Pahrump it feels like the end of the world. It's Nevada desert country, on the northwest edge of Death Valley National Park. Driving into town we pass Bride Street, Gravel Pit Road, and WTF Sand and Stone. Next to the Mobil where we gas up is a storefront church. It might have been a travel agency at one time, Anywhere But Here Travel. Now, in big letters above the door, between two crosses, the church identifies itself: IT IS FINISHED. What, as in end times?

Luigi points at the sign, gives his head an interrogative tilt.

I translate the religious text: *Siamo fritti*. Which means, roughly, in Italian: We're screwed.

The last day and a half we have defied the heat in Death Valley. Nine months ago, when I booked hotel rooms for this trip, given the choice between the Inn at the Oasis and the Ranch at Furnace Creek, I chose the Furnace. Why I do not know.

The place is more golfy than ranchy. By the looks of it, the horses have left town. Just behind the porch off our room is a blinding green lawn and what looks like a two-hole golf course. No one would be able to endure nine holes.

Nevertheless, the heat is a little bit welcome.

A few days ago, our last afternoon on the Colorado River, we plunged and splashed through eight rapids. They were not death-defying rapids, but they were fast and rough and wet, sheets of water rising over the pontoons, breaking on top of us.

When we finally hit flat water, it was pushing 3:00 p.m. We went ashore for a short hike and, using ropes and ladders, climbed up to a cave and waterfall.

Luigi and Adele have been rating waterfalls, a *cascata* (a real waterfall), a *pisciata* (a pissy little thing), a *pisciatina* (a dribble, a hardly noticeable pissy little thing). This one, tumbling into the cave from a hole twenty feet up, was anything but pissy. It was noisy, cold, and inviting. For photos, we took turns backing into it, daring each other to get wet.

Back on the raft, we swung out into the current, looking for a place to put in for the night. We needed a space wide enough and deep enough for sixteen tents, a kitchen, and two privies.

The guides know the river and the rules. We passed by a long sandy bank with a wide flat space above it. Four rafts were beached in front of it. Rule no. 1: If someone is there, keep going.

We continued down the river, passed by several more spots, all of them occupied.

The river was shaded by high cliffs. We motored downstream, all of us eager to get the hell off the raft and change into warm dry clothes. Across the bow of the raft a cool wind blew. Blew hard. We were cold. And we were wet. We passed by another spot, a space big enough for us, also occupied; two small rafts on the bank, five tents already pitched.

After twenty minutes of cold floating, our two rafts tied off each other in midstream. The guides hauled out bags of candy to pass around. We peeled wrappings off chocolate bars, off granola bars, stuffed the paper in our pockets and ate. We pulled up our collars and faced the wind, or turned our backs to it. The guides talked among themselves, probably about where to stop downstream. Rule no. 2: Don't wait too long to make camp. The candy was a distraction, and possibly a hedge against hypothermia, which takes its time but definitely had us in its sights.

When we finally pulled ashore, our space was a canyon floodplain, all rocks. Our guide apologized, said it was the best he could do. Go find your spot, he said. And we did, stumbling over rocks and uneven terrain. A little later, in a fire line, we off-loaded duffels and daybags and tents and cots and camp chairs from the rafts, and got to work.

At 5:30 the wind let up.

At 6:00 it returned, more of it.

The conch sounded at 7:00 p.m., meaning come for dinner. The guides cooked steaks, rice, warmed a green bean dish, mixed a salad. They baked two cakes. We huddled in our camp chairs, ate, and stumbled back to our tents.

Toward morning I heard coughing in the next tent. It was Adele.

I knew one of us would get sick eventually. Or more than one. And sick would present challenges. When you're sick, you want to be home. That failing, you need comfort food. You need rest. You need to be warm.

There's plenty of warm in Death Valley. At Furnace Creek, once we're checked in at the ranch, my wife and Luigi and I drive south toward Badwater Basin. Adele stays behind in their room and goes to bed, the AC turned off. Along the way we steer down into the Devil's Golf Course, get out of the car once or twice to take a picture. Those white stripes that look like water from the road above? Salt. On the display in the car, the temp reads 101.

That morning I read about how Miami is going to soon be under water. Florida newspapers have begun to make references to "the invading sea," noting: "During king tides on sunny days, seawater bubbles up through storm drains and over seawalls into lawns, streets and storefronts. That didn't happen 20 years ago, but it's going to happen more and more."

Where we are was once a sea. Now the water is deep underground, in an aquifer formed, or "charged," as geologists say, thousands of years ago, during the Pleistocene Ice Age. On the Colorado River, we struggled to face the cold. Here we struggle to face the heat.

That night we drive up to the Inn at the Oasis for dinner, looking for comfort food. The hotel is surrounded by palm trees. The grass is green, flowers abundant. The place is like a mirage.

We're seated at a table on the veranda. It wraps around the second story of the building, cooled by breezes blowing through mists drawn from groundwater on the oasis. Adele is coughing, she's headachey, she says she's not hungry. When asked, she says she would eat soup. There is no soup on the menu. She confers with my wife for a minute, then orders the campanelle in pesto. It is a fateful decision.

What comes out of the kitchen is not what she expected. The server sets down a large bowl of pasta, with four slices of mozzarella laid over the pasta, and a dozen sun-dried tomato slices mixed into the pasta, and a few forkfuls of stewed spinach adding color to the pasta. In the bottom of the bowl is a swamp of pesto.

She looks at it, aghast, spears a couple macaroni, shakes her head.

Non mi va, she says at last. I can't eat this.

She and Luigi trade looks, shake their heads. *Troppo lavorato*, she says about the pasta. I would translate this statement as follows: too much crap in it.

Luigi has rice on his plate. He scrapes half of it onto a clean salad plate for her. When my turn comes to taste the pasta dish, I sink a fork into it. Not just bad. It's world-class bad.

The next day, on the road across the desert, we practice useful Anglo-Saxon terms to describe what ails Adele and the symptoms. *Tosse* (cough). *Catarro* (phlegm). *Starnuto* (sneeze). *Brividi* (chills). *Stanchezza, fiacco* (fatigue). Our next stop is Yosemite. On our way out of the desert Luigi navigates with phone, with map, and looks at me with disbelief when, in the middle of nowhere, I turn on Trona Road. It's two lanes, no center line. It will go forty miles across the desert.

"It's not on the map," he says.

I've never been this deep in the middle of nowhere. I stop the car in the middle of the road—it's a safe bet we will not see any other cars—and look at the Rand McNally folded in his lap.

"There," I say. A faint gray line. It will take us across Searles Valley, past Fish Rocks, past Atolia, past Kramer Junction, to 395. What I need to explain is, I've never been here before, but I know where I'm going.

While we idle, a coyote walks across the road, five feet in front of us. It looks up at us and turns *toward* the car. It's a female. The heat must be killing it. We've got water in the car, we've got bread.

"No," my wife says. "Don't feed the animals."

At Yosemite the waterfalls are gigantic and in full roar. At the hotel buffet the night we arrive, Adele goes to the salad bar, where there is soup. It's vegetable, sort of like a minestrone. I know it can be terrible, a mix of leftovers and, worst of all, lots of herbs and spices to fancy it up. *Troppo lavorato.*

She lifts a spoon to her mouth and tastes. "Buona," she says.

Yes, good.

River, mountains, desert—it's what we've come for.

35 / But Why Florida?

Lately I have not lasted very long, reading on a Kindle in bed at night.

I wake up early, at 4:00 a.m., rested and happy to awake and face the day. Through the morning and afternoon we walk a lot, in weather that has been partly cold and occasionally rainy. At lunch the wine pours have been generous. By evening, approaching 10:00 p.m., it stands to reason that I'm running on empty. A page or two into whatever I'm reading (a Kate Atkinson novel right now) and I tend to nod off.

These last new nights, overtaken by nods, I've had black-and-white hallucinations, seeing things on my Kindle screen as my eyes close. These are fleeting, pixilated visions on the device's paperwhite background. Twice now, in black silhouette I've seen Florida, the distinct shape of that state, just the way it looks on the map. For a couple seconds the peninsula comes into view, then disappears.

It's a mini-dream, a flash dream. Is it about an obsession? an unfulfilled desire? About stress and deep-seated conflict? Or is it just a random, flickering reflection of a present or past experience (map study in the fifth grade, let's say), signifying nothing?

In *Medical News Today* these hallucinations are described as "hypnogogic" events, pertaining to that eerie threshold period between wakefulness and sleep. A shallow dream state. Everyone has experienced the hypnogogic jerk—barely asleep you dream that you slip, stumble on a stairstep, fall off a bicycle, and suddenly you jerk back into a wakeful state. Maybe this hallucination is akin to that.

But why Florida?

I've been to Florida exactly three times. The first time, some forty years ago, my wife and I had been married barely a year. Her parents were acquiring an investment property in Homosassa Springs. It was new construction. She and I flew down to make some decorating decisions. Not that we had any expertise in the matter. We spoke English. That was enough.

The weekend is a blur. My most vivid memory is standing on a bridge in a wildlife park, looking down at a hippo, up to its knees in a creek, gazing up at us, its mouth yawning open like the trunk of a Buick with teeth. I'm pretty sure I swam somewhere that weekend. My wife did not.

In the decades that followed, if I suggested we go to Florida, she would say no. In the cold months I would think, Why not?

"It's hot down there," she'd say.

"Isn't that the point?"

"And humid."

"Swimming pool. Ocean. Sun."

"It's hot down there."

One year, after our daughter and her husband spent a long weekend in Florida, eating in good restaurants, I got the bug again. Somehow I sold my wife on Miami, South Beach. It was January.

"A short flight," I said.

"It's hot down there."

"Art nouveau."

She thought about this one.

"Same time zone," I said.

"It's humid."

"Good restaurants," I said, "We could give it a try."

She gave her consent. The next three days she watched me swim in the ocean from the beach.

"Come on in," I said.

"It's cold."

"You get used to it."

"My feet will get all sandy."

Toweling off later, I said, "At least the restaurants are good."

"Beh," she said. I had learned enough Italian to understand "beh" means many things, among them: Don't get me wrong, I love you, and I know this frolic in the ocean is your idea of a good time, but it's definitely not mine. And as far as the restaurants go, beh.

Another fleeting memory of that weekend was water in the city. I think it was global warming aggravated by rain and high tide. In a low-lying zone one morning, as we walked past one art nouveau treasure after another, lakes began to form in intersections.

"You see," my wife said.

"Let's just cross the street."

"Another reason not to come to Florida."

"At least," I said, "we can have a nice swim this afternoon."

An observation that did not even warrant a beh.

This week we see in the news that Venice is suffering historic flooding, three days of *acqua alta* (high water). Saint Mark's Square closes. Eighty percent of the city is underwater. Images show tourists up to their thighs in water, Venetians in their sturdy hip boots.

Twenty years ago we were in Venice when the water levels rose. The elevated sidewalks were brought out. Vendors sold colorful boots, little more than yellow and blue plastic bags with soles on the bottoms and string ties above the knee. That day the *acqua alta* came and went. The locals were philosophical about the situation. "When you're in Venice, it's just a fact of life," they said. The water receded. Life returned to normal. Last year in November we were standing in Saint Mark's and the water came bubbling out of the drains in the square. An hour later it was three inches deep. A few hours after that there was six inches of water. We walked around it, got back to our hotel. Next day the city was dry.

This year feels different. Something tells me that within a few weeks, the infrastructure in Venice will be patched together again. Lights will work. Phones will ring. Hotels and restaurants will be dried up and open. The lagoon boats delivering bulk foods and table linens, transporting building material and picking up garbage, they will all run again. Gondoliers will haunt the bridges and direct visitors to their expensive canal tours. But it's hard not to be shaken. How long before the damage is irreversible, if it isn't already?

Years ago I read Susanne Langer's *Philosophy in a New Key*. Very little of it stuck with me. But what did was her discussion of the symbolic transformation of experience. All day long stuff happens to us, we are flooded with sensations, experience, and meaning. The mind processes the experience, stores it in memory, in code—images, words, figures, sounds—in symbols that we access and organize, and shape and reshape into meaning. We live in a swell, a tide of significance that rises, envelopes us.

But dreams? Langer writes, "The activity of the mind seems to go on all the time, like that of the heart and lungs and viscera; but during sleep it serves no practical purpose. . . . At best it presents us with the things we do not want to think about, the things which stand in the way of practical living."

Typically I don't think much about my dreams. For a while I had a recurring dream, vivid and disconcerting, of sitting on the toilet in my driveway in broad daylight. (I suppose it would have been just as disconcerting at night.) This dream served no practical purpose.

Two or three nights in a row I see Florida. Is my mind, or my Kindle, trying to tell me something? "Things we don't want to think about." Such as Venice going under.

Last night, same experience, different image. In a flash dream I saw a horse's head. Will I see it tonight? I hope so. But it's very possible I will go to sleep thinking about Florida.

36 / Coffee Ma'am

"I'm the coffee man," I say to my wife.

We're sitting in the kitchen, enjoying our view of the snow. It's midmorning, a single digit above zero out there, which is bad; but also out there are bright sun on new snow and a brilliant cloudless blue sky, which is good. We're well into SAD season, long stretches of short gray days, then darkness. Sun is the best antidote to Seasonal Affective Disorder. When I mentioned SAD to a friend the other day, I said sun and red wine. He smiled and said Florida is the best antidote.

Later today we're flying to Shanghai, to visit our kids. We're both a little off balance (cranky), nervous about the long flight (about fourteen hours), the time change (twelve hours), and the bad air in Shanghai. It will be cold there, damp, gray Chinese cold. China will be almost as SAD as Michigan. Maybe SADDER.

"I'm the coffee man," I say again, trying to lighten the mood. I tell her she could call me that.

She shakes her head.

I take a cup down from the cupboard and show her. She gives me an approving nod.

"'Hey, coffee man.'"

She looks away. "I won't say that."

"Try it. 'Hey, coffee man.'"

I press a button, our machine groans, and I get a nice espresso.

"Don't forget," she says, "I need toothpaste."

I remember. Later today we're going to her dentist to pick up a tube of toothpaste. My wife and I have his and hers toothpastes. I'm a traditionalist. Whatever Crest is on the shelf, I buy it and use it. At Costco you can buy a five-year supply of Crest at bargain prices and never run out.

Okay, Crest is like the Gallo of the toothpaste industry. But still, I mean, toothpaste.

My wife, on the other hand, is non-traditional. She uses a healthpaste she gets from her holistic dentist. I don't knock it. I just don't understand it. It's toothpaste. Unlike Costco, her dentist doesn't do bulk. More than a few times she's come up short and had to use the default industrial paste, which she finds abrasive.

Last night we had a shouting match about toothpaste. Not shouting in anger. Shouting across a distance—because she talks to me from wherever in the house she happens to be at that moment and I should be able to hear her. She says I'm getting deaf (true); I say where in the house are you talking to me from right now?

I was in the kitchen washing a dish when I heard her say something from a bedroom upstairs, at a far end of the house. It's where I pile stuff before I pack, on our son's bed. I thought she said why did I get the new toothpaste.

I yelled up at her: "So I can brush my teeth in Shanghai." I knew just the sight of a tube of Crest would irk her. I thought I concealed it in the pile next to some socks.

She says, "What about me?"

"What about you?"

"What about me?"

"You can use some if you need to brush your teeth."

"What?"

"I said you can use it."

"Where did you get it?"

"I got it at Kroger," I yelled back.

"At Kroger?"

"I bought it at Kroger, where they sell toothpaste. Remember last night I went to the store for milk. Well I bought milk, Benadryl, and toothpaste."

I hear her coming down the stairs now. She says, "Why did you need a new suitcase?"

"Suitcase? I thought you said toothpaste. It's toothpaste for Shanghai."

"But the suitcase. Isn't that a new suitcase?"

"No, it isn't." It wasn't. But the tube of toothpaste was new. I didn't hear clearly. Or she didn't speak clearly.

At her dentist later that morning, while she stocks up on one tube of toothpaste, I look at some holistic medical literature the dentist has on display. This stuff kills me. One particular flyer is for a product called "Olive Gold 03." It's a lotion, "the result of Research, Refinement and Development Accumulated over 125 years." Wow, that's a long time.

Olive Gold 03 (Why not just 3 instead of 03? Is 03 a year?) is available in a four-ounce container, with a pump. There's a list of ingredients, and this blandishment: "A touch of the Garden of Eden and the Fountain of Youth!" Also this: "It's Like Having an ANGEL in a BOTTLE." A few publications are cited to validate the science: *Textbook of Medical Physiology*, *Journal of Experimental Medicine*, and *Flood Your Body with Oxygen*.

On the reverse side in nine-point font is a full page of testimonials—useful in some branches of science and the healing arts, especially in the total absence of data. My favorite: GREAT FOR PETS! CRUELTY FREE! HAS A REFRESHING SCENT TOO!

Sitting by the cashier window is an old couple, both of them wearing pink sweaters against the cold, cold day. I want to ask them if they color coordinate every morning. They have a few years on my wife and me, but I know that's where we're heading. Old. In sweaters. Definitely not matching. If we can't do "coffee man," there's no way we'll wear matching sweaters.

The flight is long. We depart four hours late. Once they dim the lights my wife leans into the window and sleeps. It's a little bit of chivalry on my part, giving her the window. But also I've never been able to sleep much on a long flight, maybe because I'm not seated next to the window. Out over the ocean, wide awake, I entertain myself by watching other people's movies. Look, there's Kate McKinnon. On another screen, Jane Fonda. On another, Meryl Streep in *Mamma Mia*. Meryl is bouncing on a fluffy bed, acting so girlish and gleeful I have to look away. Some guy is watching *Ant-Man*.

When I check the flight tracker, we're flying at forty thousand feet over what must be Siberia. It's 72 below outside. The only city shown on the map is Yakutsk. Which must mean something like Yak-ville. I wonder how SAD it is down there.

Without a Benadryl assist I drift off for a short sleep, only to awaken to a flight attendant saying to my wife, "Coffee ma'am? Coffee ma'am?"

My wife is awake. She declines the coffee, but I say yes, I would love some. I turn to her, think about saying who I am, then decide against it.

37 / In Search Of

Yakgurt.

There is such a thing, tasting more of gurt than of yak. We came to Yunnan province and the city of Lijiang hoping to see, among other things, yak in the flesh, the great furry, horned beast. We did not come close, but it felt like we did.

This was a trip that began with something of a fool's errand, which led us to serendipitous yak. After we checked into our hotel in Lijiang, our kids did what they usually do—did, it could be said, what they learned from us to do—look for a good place to eat.

We left the hotel in the late afternoon with two restaurants to choose from. And set out to find choice number one.

"What's it called?" I asked my son-in-law.

He said he didn't know. Nicholas, the guy at the desk, couldn't remember the name. But it was supposed to be good.

"How will we find it?"

"It's supposed to be nearby."

I think he had the name of some roads that Nicholas had written in Chinese characters. And a vague description of the place: wood, eat upstairs.

Living in Shanghai for close to two years, my son-in-law now speaks pretty good Chinese. *Speaks.* To a nonspeaker like me, he speaks impressively, miraculously. But his is Chinese by mouth and ear, not by hand and eye. I wondered if he could match the characters Nicholas had written on a sheet of paper with street names we passed. In my total ignorance all the characters look the same. We would ask for the place we could not name. We would look for that restaurant using its physical description . . . wood, eat upstairs.

We looked. For about two hours we looked. Everyone we stopped for help glanced at Nicholas's characters and pointed in various directions. We set off in various directions, eager, hungry, confused.

Picture a maze. Now put a series of canals throughout this maze, canals twelve to seventy-two inches wide and running with fresh cold water. Everywhere you are in the old city of Lijiang you hear the sound of water—soothing, easeful, burbling water. Cobblestone streets, 250 bridges, and gardens. Gardens more of the vegetable than the flower variety. And temples and water wheels and a gazillion tourists (it was a few days before Chinese New Year). And horses? Yes, those, too, many of them, with jangling bells worn around their necks. And street food. Glorious and in all likelihood *perilous* street food for a Westerner. Bread is bread. Meat on a stick is meat on a stick. Unless it's fried duck intestine on a stick. How do you say that in Chinese? What's the character for intestine?

We looked, we inquired, we did not find the unnamed wood restaurant somewhere around there with dining upstairs. At last, exhausted and hungry, we stopped in front of a Tibetan restaurant, where we enjoyed a yak hotpot. The specialty of the house.

"It's chewy," my wife said to our daughter.

"I can't pick it up," I said, fumbling my chopsticks.

"This is so COOL," the four-year-old grandson said.

The server brought greens, mushrooms, and sprouts to the table, to souse and cook in the hotpot, and then a platter of yak sausage and yak bacon, to cook around the edges of the pot.

A hotpot and its heat source can be likened to a campfire in the middle of your table. In the pot, steaming yak broth. Around the perimeter of the fire, a strip of metal three inches wide, essentially a griddle in a circle.

"You don't eat that yak," our daughter said, pointing with a chopstick, "the yak in the pot, I mean." She lifted a strip of fried yak bacon, laid it between two pieces of soft bread, dunked it in a spicy sauce, took a bite. "Delicious," she said.

We were happy. Yak bacon and sausage sputtered, guttering in accumulated melted fat.

"I can't pick anything up," I said, fumbling my chopsticks.

Yak, I am pleased to discover, is the name of an English rock band. Their genre is described as "indie, alternative, and noise." It is also, of course, a great beast that can be domestic, numbering in the millions, and wild, numbering between twelve and fifteen thousand. The domestic creature will weigh anywhere from five hundred to thirteen hundred pounds. The wild animal does not consent to being weighed. Don't try coaxing it to the scales.

We were in wild yak country.

Next day we hiked the Yak Meadow on Snow Mountain, where we were told we might encounter yak of the wild variety. It was a long bus ride up to the ski lift that would take us on a long ride up to the trail head.

On the bus, rounding a curve we saw sheep standing in a meadow.

"Yaks!" yelled the four-year-old.

Chorus: Those aren't yaks.

At another curve we saw goats standing in a meadow.

"Yaks!" yelled the four-year-old.

Chorus: Those aren't yaks.

Another curve. We saw cows. Large animals with horns. Yak-like. But, still, cows.

"Yaks!" yelled the four-year-old.

My daughter leaned close to me, quoting her *Saturday Night Live*. "He's got a fever. And the only cure is more yak."

Would we find yak? What is a day without yak? As luck would have it, somewhere that morning, while my wife and I were lost in the maze, she had picked up some yak milk candy. She was feeding it to the baby. No one else would try it.

"It makes his breath stink," my daughter said.

Later, at the top of ski lift, we dismounted at the beginning of the Yak Meadow trail. We read this sign to the four year old: "Yak will hurt you please don't close to."

Delightful syntax mangle. Fearful message, which sort of freaked the boy out.

In the end we were in no danger. The wild yaks, our guide told us, move around with changes in the weather. They had probably gone to higher ground in search of open space and yak quietude. Leaving behind many yak muffins near and along the trail, which the grandson, avid about poop, thoroughly enjoyed.

A few days later, in another section of old Lijiang, we have a hot lunch: spicy beef, spicy noodles, spicy cucumbers, spicy cabbage, and a few other spicy dishes. At the end of such a meal you have a ring of fire around your lips; your mouth is a hotpot all its own. There is one thing will control the burn: yakgurt.

Think frozen yogurt, only with more density, probably more milk fat, a cold convection with the consistency of putty, in a cone or cup. We went with the cup. The baby ate it, avid about his yak. His dad ate it. I ate it.

We came, we did not close to. Nonetheless we felt yakked.

38 / The Efficacy of Loud

The bar is called Speak Low, on Fuxing Middle Road in Shanghai.

My daughter and I have come here on a Saturday night for a few cocktails. This is the third F&B joint (Food and Bar) I've been to. All three with ground level entrance, little more than an anteroom with space for a desk and two greeters, and a door that leads to a stairway that leads to second, third, and fourth floor rooms with bars, tables, low light, and a lot of noise. The room we're in is full of youngish people—tables and chairs for thirty or so—maybe seventy-five people total seated and standing. They have shiny new shoes, important hair, and serious glasses. Shanghai chic. This might as well be Brooklyn.

"I'd like the old-fashioned," I tell our server.

She nods and says in English that the drink comes with . . . something.

"What?" It's noisy. And I am hard of hearing.

Something, she says again. It comes with something.

I make a face indicating that one of us is stupid and it's definitely not her.

"Bacon," my daughter says at last. "Your drink comes with bacon."

Bacon? In the drink or beside the drink? I would sort of like an explanation. And is it bacon bacon or yak bacon?

My daughter orders a celery gimlet for herself.

I'd like to ask our server to explain the name of the bar, Speak Low. Were they aiming for Speak Easy? If so, I'm glad they muffed it. Speak Low is odd, and exotic, and, given the ambiance, contradictory. Tonight Speak Low's patrons are definitely speaking high. My daughter and I are not talking to each other. We are yelling.

After a second drink I find my way to the restroom, prepared to use the two words of Chinese that I know.

There's one door. No words in English, no Chinese characters, no icons on the door. So: coed. The door is not ajar. It's closed. I wait a minute. Then another minute. When at last I knock and pull the door open, two women at the one sink turn and look at me in surprise. Behind them, two doors, open, behind which business is transacted.

I would like to say excuse me. That's what I would say at home. Unfortunately those are not my two words in Chinese.

"Nihao," I say instead. Hello. Feeling pretty stupid, I shut the door on them, out of respect. After a minute they push the door open and step out.

I would still like to say excuse me.

"Xiexie," I say instead. Thank you.

I may be stupid, but at least I'm polite about it.

This is my second trip to Shanghai. This time around Speak Low is a resonant term. Also a misnomer of sorts. Who speaks low? In forty-eight hours I've gotten an earful of Chinese.

On the flight over, the carrier in Detroit filled up with Chinese people going directly to Shanghai. They looked like some serious Chinese, the clothes, the walk, the flat expressions; like people who live in China, not Plymouth, and were going home. Behind my wife and me a couple took their seats and began immediately to talk in Chinese. Mostly loud animated explanations. Mostly the man talking to the woman. They talked loud nonstop for the next thirteen hours of the thirteen-hour nonstop flight. Before takeoff, through the dinner service, as we crossed the Bering Sea passing into deep darkness, through the wake-up meal and snack that followed, and while the cabin crew prepared the cabin for landing and advised us that our luggage in the overhead might have shifted, this couple yakked and yelled at each other.

"What could they possibly be talking about?" I murmured to my wife.

She rolled her eyes and slumped against her window. "Just ignore them."

Impossible.

When I told my daughter about the pair she nodded and said people talk like that—speak loud—over here.

Next day, in front of our grandson's preschool, one of the six guards standing out front verbally attacked a car that pulled up and parked wrong. At least I think that's what was going on. One guard leaned over and yelled through the open window at the driver. The driver yelled back. They could have been talking about the weather.

At the grocery store next to the kids' apartment, where I went for a liter of milk, the noise was deafening, women shouting at each other over bok choy and mushrooms, possibly just making loud small talk, swapping recipes, but to my ear, it was an auditory episode of mortal combat.

From the sidewalk you can hear the yelling inside food stalls. What's up?

Personal space varies from one culture to another, something Sting posited (see: "Don't Stand So Close to Me"). Americans like to maintain a certain distance—four to five feet—between speakers; Chinese speakers are less inclined to do so. Perhaps in like fashion, one culture is more tolerant of loud talk than the other.

The Sinology Institute describes the four tones common to spoken Chinese, noting: "If you put the 'high voice' (first tone) and 'suspicious voice' (2nd tone) together with the fourth tone (anger), then there are 85 percent of tones in Mandarin Chinese that may sound unhappy and aggressive and make you feel uneasy."

It's all about what I would call the efficacy of loud.

Evan Osnos, in *Age of Ambition: Chasing Fortune, Truth, and Faith in the New China*, devotes part of a chapter to Li Jang, a popular—and highly successful and extremely rich—English teacher. (Yes, you read that right.) His winning and evidently highly effective teaching principle is "English as a shouted language." Li stumbled upon his approach when studying for a language proficiency exam he had already failed once. Osnos writes that Li "studied for [the] exam by reading aloud and found the louder he read, the bolder he felt and the better he spoke." Li's shouting technique, he believes, unleashes "the international muscles."

If I weren't distracted by eels, dried ducks, and pig faces as I walk the neighborhood, I might dedicate myself to vocabulary acquisition. Learning one word a day, by the end of this trip I would have twenty new words. That's a 1,000 percent increase in vocabulary. I figure it's not too late to start.

Lu. That's the Chinese word for road. Speak Low is on Fuxing Lu. To take possession of the word, however, I shouldn't say it like a midwestern American. I should say it loud. Lu!

This morning I order coffee at Pain Chaud, a cool French pastry and coffee shop next door. Yes, French. Adding to the linguistic confusion. Nihao! I thunder when the little barista greets me. She's French and looks at me like I'm nuts. Xiexie! for the coffee, I shout when the little Chinese girl sets my cup on the counter. She ducks for cover, behind her giant espresso machine.

The approach will take some practice. It would help if I had five or ten more words. But it's a start.

And using Chinese as a shouted language is better than being meek and misunderstood. Maybe by the end of the trip I'll be standing in the middle of the Lu! exercising my international muscles.

39 / Yoga, Space, and Bragadin's Skin

"I like the albumin," I say to my wife.

We're having a light breakfast before going to yoga. I'm one egg, sunny side up; she's two eggs, poached. I tried yoga with her a year ago, half a dozen sessions, and decided it was too much work. Plus, it's a full hour of listening and following directions, which is probably good discipline, but still, it's discipline. I'm trending post-discipline these days. But she's persuaded me to give it another try. The mind-body connection appeals to me, or the idea of it does. Today will be my fourth session.

"You mean the white," she says. "And I think it's AL-bu-min. Accent on the first syllable."

I'm an al-BU-min man myself. Always have been. I tell her this.

"Like LE-panto," she says. Like this: LAY-pon-toh. "Or like that city near Cinque Terre."

"Levanto," I say. Like this: LAY-von-toh. One year we had rabbit for lunch in Levanto after a hike across the hills from Monterosso. I remind her now of that day.

We pause for bites of egg. I'm remembering that hike above the sea, the rabbit, and the pasta with pesto that came before the rabbit. I can tell she's thinking, but probably not about that lunch. A while back she read a book and subsequently had a lot to say at the breakfast table about Lepanto and the Ottoman-Venetian War in the 1500s. I'm pretty sure she'll go there.

"Al-BU-min." I say it my way, picking up my phone. "Let's ask Jeeves how to say that."

"Lepanto," she says again.

While I'm searching for pronunciation help (more like confirmation help, as I'm pretty sure I'm right) I remind her our daughter hates the word albumin. And lunchmeat. You can't get her to say albumin or lunchmeat. Either, ever. While I scroll, my wife revisits what she read about Lepanto, a city in the south of Italy, and the siege of Famagusta, and that Venetian captain, Marcantonio Bragadin, who was skinned alive. "Flayed," she says, daubing yolk with some bread. The Turks, she adds, kept Bragadin's skin, stuffed it with straw, and paraded him around the streets of Famagusta, and then took the skin with them back to Constantinople.

"So rude," I say. I show her my phone. "It's al-BU-min."

"After the Battle of Lepanto," she says, "the Italians recovered Bragadin's skin and returned him to Venice."

We get to yoga early enough for a long warm-up. For me that's lying on the floor, on my mat, on my back, my head on a rolled-up towel pillow. Eyes closed, I pay attention to my breathing: That's the putative reason for just lying there: A mindful warm-up. Letting my mind wander is the real reason. It's a peaceful, fanciful moment. A few feet away my wife stretches. A few more feet away a guy our age stretches in earnest, stretches and moans; moans in kind of a sexual sounding way, which, to me, seems uncalled for.

Then Kadesha breezes in. She's dressed in dark green tights, a sleeveless camouflage pullover, her straight reddish hair pulled back in a ponytail. She rolls out her mat, lowers the lights in the room, starts the mood music. I'm guessing Kadesha is forty-something. She's been in the United States long enough to speak perfect English, but with a yoga-appropriate accent. (She says "wortabrae," which I love.) She's also pliable as a rubber band. Try the poses, she says. But don't hurt yourself.

We do a few warm-ups. We go through a series of dog poses. Down dog, up dog, bird dog, three-legged dog, extended puppy, playful puppy. Then we transition to mountain pose and some of the warrior poses. I never knew my arms weighed so much. At regular junctures she reminds us keep the mind-body connection in mind. On one hand, that's easy, especially when fatigue and pain come into play, which is often. Body is all you can think about then. On the other hand, the mind can wander off. Mine does.

This morning, it wanders to the Mueller report and, specifically, to two spaces.

Everyone is riled up about the Mueller report. Earlier today a new, and odd, grievance surfaced in my reading. Writing for the *Philadelphia Inquirer*, the Angry Grammarian (a.k.a. Jeffrey Barg), observed: "The attorney general of the United States has just executed a cover-up so brazen, so grotesque, so audacious, that it was done in plain view. Right under our noses. He put two spaces after his periods."

Ouch, lord-of-the-fishes pose.

We're fifteen minutes into the session. I'm hot, out of breath, and weak. Rest anytime you like, Kadesha says.

Two spaces, I think. That's what I do. I took typing from Mrs. Darwin in the tenth grade. In a room with seats and desks and machines for thirty kids, half the typewriters were manual, half were electric. There must have been a coin toss at the beginning of the semester, or maybe it was the tyranny of alphabetical order. I had to start on a manual, which was terrible. Not exactly finger yoga, but something like that. You pounded out p's and ?'s, shifts and returns with your right pinkie, tabbing and shifting and smashing q's and z's with your left pinkie. Every day I looked across the room, eager to go electric. Like any beginning typist, I looked at QWERTY and thought, What the hell? Wasn't there an easier way to arrange the letters?

Revolved side angle pose.

You expect me to look at the ceiling, Kadesha. Really?

That was 1968. For roughly the next three decades I space-spaced after every sentence on my manual Olivetti and then electric Smith Corona typewriter. I continued to do so when I transitioned to the computer. I *type* on my computer. There's never been a substitute for that antiquated verb. I don't word process or keyboard. I type.

In yoga, you think once you get on the floor, the work will be a little easier. At minimum, there is less risk of falling over. Lord-of-the-dance pose? Extended-hand-to-big-toe pose? These are invitations to collapse. But on the floor is not easier. Definitely not. Side-plank combines the agony of plain plank with impossible equilibrium challenges. Lord-of-the-fishes pose? Noose pose? Just kill me.

Space-space is all about the transition from monospacing to proportional fonts. In Mrs. Darwin's (and my) world, every letter, number, and mark of punctuation took up the same space on the page. After a period, space-space broke up the text, giving the reader's eyes a rest, clearly demarcating sentence as segment, unit of thought and meaning. Eventually it just became what you did. Space-space. Next sentence. It was automatic. Then came computers and fonts that allocated just the right amount space, proportional to the skinny characters (i, l, !) and the fat characters (W, Y, T).

Cow pose, okay. I like this one, Kadesha.

Bow pose? Probably not in this lifetime.

People are surprisingly passionate about the space-space thing. Farhad Manjoo, writing for *Slate*: "Typing two spaces after a period is totally, completely, utterly, and inarguably wrong." Megan McCardle, opining in the *Atlantic*: "You can have my double space when you pry it from my cold, dead hands."

Forty-five minutes on, I've had about enough and sink into child's pose. It's where I feel comfortable. Sheepish, but earnestly relaxed. For the last few minutes I drop in and drop out of poses. I'm a work in progress. Finally, Kadesha rolls us on our backs, for the five-minute relax and meditate at the end of the session. Five-minute mind wander. I lie there, breathe, and wonder: Can I reprogram myself, transition from space-space to space? Should I?

"How was it?" my wife asks later. We're walking out to the parking lot.

"Murder," I say.

"Good for your core," she says. "Good for your back."

We ride home, at peace with our thoughts, stretched and fatigued. I tell her briefly about the space-space controversy. Attorney General Barr's four-page letter, some crank noted, would have been three and a half pages without two spaces after periods. How about that?

"Why does it matter?"

"It doesn't," I say. "I'm old-school. Two spaces. I bet you are too."

She says she's never thought about it.

"Bragadin's skin," she says after a short pause (more than two spaces), "is in one of the churches in Venice. On display."

"That's gross."

"It's history."

"You Italian Catholics and your relics," I say.

"We should find out which church it's in," she says. It's an invitation—for me to ask Jeeves.

"Is it framed?"

She rolls her eyes. "Next time we go to Venice, I want to see Bragadin's skin."

Next yoga session, she tells me, on Tuesdays with Tina, is different. Tina walks around the room most of the time. She will occasionally correct your posture.

"You mean I'm doing it wrong?" I say. I'm sure that I am. If correction means less pain, I'm all for it. Somehow I doubt that will be the case. Doing it right can only mean more pain.

I picture the two of us in the room, along with the moaning guy and the rest of the class, holding our poses, forming geometric shapes and letters of the alphabet with our bodies. I know it's important to get things right in the beginning, not to form bad habits. A bad habit can last forever.

40 / Don't Wait

My wife and I are having breakfast one morning in northwest Detroit. It's a bar/restaurant. On a couple big-screen TVs, highlights from last night's baseball games play. Sawing on a piece of avocado toast, for which they have given me a steak knife, I look up and admire assorted junk and portraiture on the walls—a few famous locals (Madonna, Robin Williams) and a few famous not locals (Winston Churchill, Albert Einstein). Above the photos and hanging bric-a-brac and do-dads loom the heads of great beasts—elk and caribou, a moose, a few deer and antelope that play no more.

"Do you think they vacuum those heads?" I say.

She doesn't look up. She's been listening in on the conversation of two guys sitting a few tables over from us. She's asked me a couple times, Did you hear that? Did you hear that?

No, I didn't. There's too much circumambient noise.

(The only good thing about gradual hearing loss is the gradual increase in your opportunity to use the word "circumambient.")

In fact, she's a little irritated with me at the moment. We had just placed our order with the server when, looking over my head toward the back of the restaurant, my wife said, "Look at that [something or other] hanging there."

Something or other. I didn't turn and look. I just said what I sort of heard. "Chainsaw?"

"Chandelier," she says, louder.

In situations like this, a word can be a Rorschach test, an auditory blob. You make of it what you will.

"Those animal heads up there," I say, nodding in their direction, "they must be loaded with dust."

"I have to wonder about you," she says. "Doesn't it bother you that you can't hear? I'm amazed, the things you say when I ask you a question. Chainsaw, really?"

"Too much circumambient noise," I say. I tell her I was just having fun.

"It's not fun," she says.

We both take bites and chew. She turns her head slightly, listening. The two guys, I hear now, are talking about dementia.

I ask her: "Do you think there's a service? A guy in a van with specialized equipment, he travels around the Detroit area vacuuming animal heads hung up in restaurants and bars?"

She doesn't answer. She heard what I said. I know she did.

"Moose heads," I say. "I wouldn't want to sit under one of those. All that dust."

"Really," she says. "Doesn't it bother you? Not hearing?"

Moose dusting. It would not be a growth industry. More of a niche thing. But you have to figure, steady work. Dust, after all, is a constant. To her point, I say, yes, it does bother me, but not as much as the thing on my foot.

"What is it?"

I lightly grind the toes of my right foot into the floor, feeling for the spot. "What it is is this little thing," I say, "something growing on the bottom of my foot."

Back home, pleased that I've remembered one important thing, I do a search for "double verbs" to see what I can find out about the "is is" "was was" sentence. I had a co-worker who used is is and was was in sentences all the time. "What it is is an opportunity to write a grant and get some money." "What it was was a complete change in the way the workplace was organized."

First hit I click is for double modals: might could, should oughta, musta coulda, used to could. I decide I best keep looking. Second hit, a Washington State University professor describes is is as a colloquialism, a verbal stumble that occurs when a speaker loses track in the middle of a sentence. A stumble. Or, if you're not losing track, if you're doing it on purpose, it may be just an odd little verbal curlicue.

My search reveals that people are far less interested in "is is" than they are in "it is what it is." This, from the Urban Dictionary: "It is what it is. Used often in the business world, this incredibly versatile phrase can be literally translated as 'fuck it.'"

A variant comes to mind, from my distant past.

In the spring of 1980, when I taught eighth grade English for a semester at Post Middle School, I had a student named Rodney who greeted me every morning with What it is! He struggled with my name, he called me Mr. Barley for a few weeks, but eventually he got it. What it is, Mr. Bay-LEE! he would say. Every morning I looked forward to it. What it is, Mr. Bay-LEE! And I would answer, What is it, Rodney. I sometimes think my life would not have been complete without that salutation. It was more than what it was. What it was was really cool.

Next morning in the dermatologist's waiting room, after completing the information form and describing the purpose of my visit ("a thing on my foot") I'm pleased to find an old issue of the *New Yorker* among the golf magazines. As usual there are two poems in the issue. Also as usual, there's one I somewhat like and one I don't understand and therefore do not like. I don't understand in the sense of: what the hell is the poet saying, and who cares? And why does the *New Yorker* publish stuff like this? The poem I like is about death. It takes up part of two pages in the magazine, which is a long time to stay with death in the *New Yorker*. But the poet makes it worth my while. And the poem makes a good point. Death sucks.

Setting the magazine aside, I wonder why I waited so long before coming to the doctor. What little wisdom I've come to as an older person could be summed up in two words: don't wait. The thing on my foot is probably a wart. I picture it down there, just south of my toes, like a weed putting down roots, slowly growing. A slow burgeoning. I wonder if there's a thing like Round Up, a serum Monsanto has engineered, a dab of which wipes out the wart, root system and all.

When I was in the fourth grade in Mrs. Mann's room, I sat next to Forrest Whitman. He had a wart on his right hand, between his index and middle fingers. It was almost the size of a pea, black and kind of crusty and, well, warty. It looked like an old wart. And on such a young person. He told me one day that his mother had warned him not to pick at it. If he did, he could get cancer. For months now—that's how long I've had this thing on my foot—I've avoided picking at it. Not because of Forrest Whitman's mother. More because my father always used to say to me and my brother, about whatever anomalous thing we were hosting on our skin, Don't pick at it.

Also because I suspect that picking at it will stimulate growth, cause the thing's root system to expand and burgeon.

I'm thinking of picking up the *New Yorker* again when Rachel appears and takes me back to the examining room. She's dressed in medical-center burgundy and looks to be in her midfifties. She has a mass of curly reddish hair pulled back, a pair of gold rim glasses. The lenses kind of sparkle in the artificial light. She also sparkles in the artificial light. For some people she would be a little too bright and chirpy for this time of day. I don't mind.

"So fall has arrived," she says.

Yes, I say. And pumpkin pie. I tell her we're eating our first Costco pumpkin pie of the season. I was going to wait a few weeks before buying one, but then I thought, Why wait? While I get settled on the examination table, Rachel and I take turns making appreciative remarks about Costco cakes and pies (how big they are!) and the challenge of buying one if you live alone, which Rachel announces she does.

She finds me on the computer and asks the reason for my visit.

"What it is is this thing on the bottom of my foot," I say, taking self-conscious delight in the sentence.

She makes a note of the thing on my foot, hands me an alcohol swab, and invites me to clean the spot.

She squints through her glasses at it. "Probably a wart," she says.

Minutes later the doctor, whose name I already know is Doctor Johnson, introduces herself. Before looking at it, she tells me the thing on my foot may be a plantar wart, explaining briefly the meaning of the word plantar (not planter): "of or pertaining to the foot." Explaining, further, that if it is that, that she will have to burn it. I assume foot presentation posture on the examination table; she unwraps an instrument resembling an X-Acto blade and goes to work at some professional diagnostic scraping. That is to say, she picks at it.

After a minute she sits back on her stool and says, "I think it's a punctate callus."

Callus sounds good to me, better than wart. And I especially like "punctate."

"Punctate," I say.

"A spot or point," she says, "differentiated from the surrounding area." She washes her hands, tells me it still might be a wart or it might not. I should come back if the thing comes back. It was a pleasure, for her and me both.

Back home, my wife tells me she has stumbled upon an article I should read, about hearing aids that can make a fashion statement. If glasses, which correct a vision deficit, can be fashionable, why not a hearing aid, which can correct a hearing deficit? She knows I like fancy glasses, so maybe? I'm not interested, but I tell her I'll take a look, maybe a little later.

"Really?" she says.

"Really," I say.

"Really?" she says.

This is what love is—care for another that's also care for oneself.

My phone pings the arrival of the article. And her brief, loving message with it. Don't wait.

41 / Third Eye Seeing

She announced, out of nowhere, that she could see auras.

I was sitting with this girl at the Orange Julius in Ann Arbor late one afternoon in 1973. It was a sunny day in early April, the end of winter semester. Outside, the last of the blackened snow was melting.

"Around some people," she said, "I see this shimmering."

I was an undergraduate. She and I were finishing a course in metaphysical poetry together. After class that day she said she wanted to try this place on University. Would I come with her? All semester we had felt like Platonic pals. I said sure, thinking if the opportunity presented itself, just for the fun of it I might quote some Andrew Marvell to her: "Had we but world enough and time, this coyness, lady, were no crime." I wondered now if she saw my aura. Maybe she had been watching it all along.

"It tastes like an orange Creamsicle," I said. I picked up my cup, admiring the smiling Julius devil logo, gave my drink another stir with the straw, and took a sip.

"There's egg in it," she said. "That's what makes it creamy."

I told her friends of mine who took LSD said they saw auras.

"Friends," she said with a smile.

"No hallucinations. Just auras. They seemed kind of disappointed."

"This is different," she said. "I see energy fields surrounding people. Everyone has an aura. But not everyone can see them." She was looking at me, but also around me, beyond me, like over my shoulder. I thought she must be taking me in.

"That guy over there," she said, "his aura is spazzing right now." I turned to look. A little guy with big ears and matted black hair was bent over a notebook, scribbling with a pencil. She said she saw flares of energy around him, a lot of red and dense orange. "Orange is a sign of power, associated with passion and sexual energy."

"Him?" I said. I took another drink. And then another. "What about mine?" I gestured in the direction of what I imagined to be my aura. "Whatta you see?"

I thought of auras years later when I started seeing them. Up early one morning, walking downstairs in the dark, I sensed this shimmering in my field of vision. Then, sitting in the living room, drinking a cup of coffee, all around my bare feet I had propped on the ottoman I noticed what looked suspiciously like an aura. Can you see your own aura? Around your feet? I didn't think so. A little later I ate a dish of yogurt and saw its aura. When I took the garbage cans down to the road, all around them was a definite shimmering aura. The mailbox had an aura. I wanted to wake up my wife, see if she was shimmering. Maybe she would glow in the dark.

This went on for a week or so.

"It's not auras you're seeing," my wife said when I told her about it. "I think there's something wrong with your eyes."

"Auras are a thing," I said. "I knew this girl in college."

"You saw an aura around your feet? Around the mailbox? Really. You should call David."

David the ophthalmologist who lives behind us. I started to say there was more under heaven and earth, Horatio, but thought better of it. "What about your cousin's wife, the one in Switzerland with healing hands?"

She rolled her eyes, said I should just call Dave.

That afternoon in David's office, I scored low on the alphabet test. It was frustrating. I know my letters. With my right eye, *Could be a B, could be an F, might be a D*. The tech didn't say anything.

Final grades would be held until the end of the appointment. Next I got the cover test, the ocular motility test, some refraction and retinoscope work, the pressure test, the slit lamp test, and a full-blown retinal scan. And lots of drops. When I finally saw David, I told him that in the lower left quadrant of my field of vision, like six o'clock to nine o'clock, it was shimmery and shadowy. Worse now than when I came in—because of the drops. And if I turned my head, there was a band, a dark line, cutting across from eleven o'clock to two o'clock.

He said it looked like I had a torn and detached retina. Along with some schisis. That was a new word. *Schisis.* Not a word I ever wanted to know. And it sounded like he was using it in the plural.

I left his office wearing temporary sunglasses and made a shimmery drive down Telegraph Road to the Comerica Building, where a retina surgeon examined me, confirmed David's diagnosis, and scheduled surgery for me at 6:00 a.m. the next day.

I've heard of people who get hit on the head, then gifts follow. Perfect pitch. Mental telepathy. The ability to see the future. Remembering a prior life. A sudden affinity for prime numbers. In *The Man Who Mistook His Wife for a Hat*, Oliver Sacks writes about deficits and enhancements. Was I enhanced? Was aura reading in my future?

Back home I did a little research on retinas and auras. I found a page of aura reading tips. "Close your eyes, align your breath, and ask the colors to show themselves to you." This from a website called Gaia, dedicated to expanding consciousness. I tried that out, stumbling just a little on the "align your breath" part. I guessed it meant sit up straight. "Gently rub your hands together. This activates energy between the two hands and turns on the Aka." *Aka*, an ancient Egyptian term for "energy field." (So, that's "energy field," a.k.a. "Aka.") The colors, if I saw them, would invite me to feel loved and cherished or drain me of my energy.

I looked at my wife, across from me at the dinner table that night. We were finishing off some leftovers.

"Nothing to eat or drink after midnight," she said.

"I know."

"We have to be there at 5:30 a.m."

"I know."

"I'm worried."

"I know."

I felt loved and cherished. Also slightly chastened. Like I had brought auras and retina trouble upon myself.

"So we should leave the house," she said, "at a little after five."

My eyes were still dilated. She was shimmering just a little. I rubbed my hands together to get her Aka activated. No colors. Just a slight blur. But wait, was I supposed to rub my hands together or ask her to rub *her* hands together? Whose Aka was I supposed to turn on?

At 6:00 a.m. the next morning in pre-op, they started an IV and administered a low-dose anesthetic. When they rolled me into the OR a little later, I was awake. The surgeon had to drain the vitreous humor from my right eye. He had to get his laser and instruments inside my eye to patch things up. He worked; still awake, I felt free to ask questions.

"We doin' okay?" he asked.

"Yep."

"Feel that?"

"Nope."

To his assistant, he said, "That's a schisis right there. And another one there."

"How long's this take?" I asked. Usually before a surgery you get to lay eyes on the doctor. By the time he checked in I was already partially anesthetized, my face totally covered. I would have liked to look him over, check out his aura.

He said I was doing fine. Just fine.

"How soon will I be able to read? Can I still work in the kitchen? Go for a short walk on the treadmill?"

"Why don't we talk about that in the office tomorrow."

"Okay."

"See the tissue here?" he said to his assistant.

"My head feels frozen. Forehead, face, numb."

"We did that while you were asleep."

"I was asleep?"

"Long enough to administer the local."

Local. I pictured a big-ass needle stuck in my eye. "Good idea," I said.

There's a four-minute video, by a woman named Cynthia, that explains how to practice seeing auras. You start with your hand, holding it out in front of you like you're admiring your nails. You don't really look at your fingers. You look at the spaces between them, the interstitial spaces. If you don't see anything, Cynthia says to massage the middle of your forehead. That's a chakra zone. Behind that space is the pineal gland, your "third eye."

According to the Stanford Philosophy Archives, Descartes thought that your soul was located in that part of your brain, that the pineal gland was full of "animal spirits," and that these spirits were "a very fine wind, or rather a very lively and pure flame" that filled the sails of your soul. At the end of the nineteenth century, Madame Helena Petrovna Blavatsky referred to this "third eye" as the eye of Shiva and "the organ of spiritual vision."

I had my aura read in Italy a few years ago. It was an accident. I wasn't asking for it. My wife and I met a couple guys one night in a bookstore. One of them lectured on music at the university up in San Marino. The other guy, I don't know what he did for hire. He said he read auras. When he looked at me, he seemed visibly startled. He said I looked very stressed, emotionally unsettled. *Disturbato* is what he said. Maybe emotionally disturbed doesn't mean in Italian what it does in English.

I was actually having a low-level temper tantrum at the moment. It probably didn't take a third eye to notice. I remember thinking, Dude, you could keep that to yourself. Especially the *disturbato* part. I told him it must be kind of a burden seeing things in other people. What do you do with such knowledge (if that's what it is)? What I also thought was, Shouldn't you ask someone's permission before you read their aura? Then again, maybe reading is reading. You can't *not* read a word that you know. If you can read an aura, how can you not read it?

Your post-op posture after retina surgery is simple: Head down. Try to sit still. All afternoon my whole head still felt frozen, numbed. No pain. Over the next several days, my right eye was all ashimmer, all aura, no sight. If I closed my good eye this is what I saw: A gray lunar surface with a few craters here and there. Flowering bushes slightly agitated by a breeze, at twilight. A topographical map of the American Southwest; rivers and tributaries, hills and mountains, a section of which clearly looked like Texas.

"When I close my good eye," I told my wife, "I can see my pulse."

"Just hold still."

"A blood vessel in my eye is going *boing, boing, boing*."

"Please don't move your eyes."

One afternoon, I saw two bubbles, a big one and a little one, attached to each other, like they were kissing.

On the sixth day I take a few steps, keeping my good eye closed. My right eye is now like a glass of water that's half full. The surface tension wobbles with each step. Seated, I can see almost clearly in the top half of my field of vision; below the surface it's murky, opaque. I'm part land, part aquatic creature. It feels a little bit like progress.

I decide I can do without the third eye and the burden of seeing with it. I don't even want two and a half eyes.

Just give me two, or as close to that as I can get.